THE AXIS OF EVIL COOKBOOK
Gill Partington

SAQI
London San Francisco Beirut

British Library Cataloguing-in-Publication Data
A catalogue record for this book is available from the British Library

ISBN: 978-0-86356-631-8

Text copyright © Gill Partington, 2007

This edition published 2007 by Saqi

A full cip record for this book is available from the British Library
A full cip record for this book is available from the Library of Congress

Design & some recipie pics: Richo Eyes
Illustrations: Richard Henson

SAQI
26 Westbourne Grove, London W2 5RH
825 Page Street, Suite 203, Berkeley, California 94710
www.saqibooks.com

Contents

  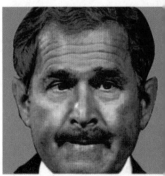

INTRODUCTION

'When I was coming up, it was us versus them, and you knew who them were,' declared President George W. Bush, with characteristic sagacity. But as the dust settled over the ruins of the Twin Towers, it was no longer clear who 'them' were. Bush realised we were facing a new and sinister enemy. It doesn't play by the rules. It doesn't even wear a uniform (although it does often tend to have a beard). Was it a 'known unknown' or an 'unknown unknown'? We just didn't know. But one thing was certain: whoever was responsible for this terrible act, they - or failing that, someone else entirely - would be held to account. And so was born the Axis of Evil ...

Iran, Iraq, North Korea, Libya, Syria, Cuba. These are the countries named in 2002 by Bush and senior White House officials as 'rogue states', outposts of tyranny and all-round enemies of democracy and wholesomeness. Threatening global stability through their acquisition of dangerous weapons and expansionist aggression, the leaders of these countries terrorise their own people with their despotic, un-elected regimes.

Along with evil also-rans like Myanmar and Belarus, this pernicious cabal represents a new threat to peace and civilisation. Admittedly it might not look like they're on the same team (and in the case of Iran and Iraq, possibly they were so preoccupied with fighting each other that they might not have been aware of it themselves), but hey, that's evil for you. It works in sinister and mysterious ways. Yep, all around the world today Satan and his hoary minions are on the march, finding a home in these diverse and far-flung places (although overall he does seem to favour hot, sandy conditions).

But what exactly have these Axis of Evil countries got to do with the much-vaunted War on Terror? Well, if you're going to split hairs, then strictly speaking, nothing. None of them have been found to be technically, directly, actually responsible for 9/11. But it was definitely the kind of thing they might have done if they'd thought of it. And obviously we can't just sit back and wait for them to not launch yet another devastating attack. That's why we need to attack them before they attack us. The logic of the pre-emptive strikes endorsed by the president's neocon advisors is so simple that an idiot can understand it: if you want peace, you need to have a war.

And who is going to combat the Axis of Evil? A mighty 'coalition of willing' consisting of the USA, Britain, Mongolia and... well that's it, really. The list may be on the short side but, quite frankly, who cares about mere mortal allies when you've got God on your side? The forces of evil can only be defeated by the forces of good, as George Bush knows only too well from his regular conversations with God.

Bush isn't the only one with a hotline to heaven, either; fundamentalist Christian White House adviser Pat Robertson also keeps in contact with the Almighty, as does the man in charge of Pentagon military plans post 9/11, Lieutenant General William Boykin. Washington might have been trying to play down the idea that this was a 'crusade', but Boykin had other ideas, declaring he was confident of victory against his Islamic opponent since 'my God is bigger than his god'. And as for those atheist commies in North Korea and Cuba, well, they don't even have a god at all!

Good always wins in the end, of course; anyone who's ever seen a war film knows that. Just to be on the safe side, though, the forces of good will be backed up with actual force, and by lots and lots of really expensive state-of-the-art weaponry. Liberating the oppressed citizens of the Axis of Evil isn't going to be easy, but having the biggest defence budget on the planet makes it a bit less daunting. And, as Bush points out, if they don't listen to reason we can just 'bomb the hell out of them'.

That's not to say President Bush embarks on military action lightly. 'War is a dangerous place,' he acknowledges, and he's a man who knows, having served in the Vietnam War. Well, strictly speaking, he wasn't actually in Vietnam; some protracted dental treatment kept him in the USA for the duration of the conflict, but still, those dentists' drills can be hazardous things in the wrong hands.

'You're either with us or against us,' according to Dubya's much-publicised maxim. And lo, all of creation was divided into two: good and evil. Even food, as Bush found to his cost when the infamous pretzel-choking incident brought him a brush with death. Food is, of course, a potent symbol; an embodiment of our way of life and freedom, and Bush is well aware that it's a subject dear to his citizens' hearts. 'I know how difficult it is for you to put food on your families,' he told baffled voters. (Luckily, he didn't have the same problem himself, regularly spraying his nearest and dearest with semi-digested pretzel. In fact, the Bush clan seem to have a somewhat chequered record in the food digestion department: Bush Sr once graciously thanked the Japanese Prime Minister for his hospitality by throwing up all over him.)

But what they lack in sophistication, Bush's tastes make up for in patriotism. He likes peanut butter and jelly sandwiches and cheese enchiladas (Mexico is part of the USA, right?), no doubt accompanied by some 'freedom fries'. Bush's stalwart ally Tony Blair is equally patriotic in his eating habits. He likes no-nonsense great British staples like fish and chips, and, er, 'fresh fettuccine garnished with an exotic sauce of olive oil, sun-dried tomatoes and capers'.

But what about their adversaries in the Axis of Evil? Even the most committed evildoers have to eat. So what does your average crazed despot have for his tea? Do they dine on the tender flesh of newborn infants or perhaps live on an exclusive diet of blueberry flavour Pop Tarts? And what do their oppressed citizens enjoy for breakfast? These outposts of tyranny are, after all, places where citizens are denied the basic human right to buy a Chicken McNugget; where burgers are outlawed on pain of death. How can humans survive such deprivation? What downright un-American things are they forced to eat? And just what does evil actually taste like? Find out before it's vanquished completely ...

Stars and Stripes Salad

You will need

1 bag (10 oz.) fresh spinach, torn into bite-size pieces

1 cup chopped onions

3 large sweet red peppers

6 hard-boiled eggs, chopped

poppy-seed dressing

So much has been said and written about the 'war on terror'. But sometimes words just aren't adequate to the task of expressing the magnitude and complexity of the conflict, the reality of war, and the terrible cost paid already by so many. So why not say it with salad? It's the low-fat way of expressing your love of freedom and democracy!

Directions

In a large bowl, mix together spinach and onions. Place salad in a 13x9-inch glass dish or plastic container. Cut off tops and bottoms of peppers; remove seeds. Cut peppers in half horizontally and remove skins. Using a 2-inch or smaller star-shaped cookie cutter, cut 5 stars from each pepper. Place pepper stars in rows of 3 down and 5 across. Place eggs in rows between the stars. Serve with poppy-seed dressing.

Iraq

It was 2003, and the Taliban had been overthrown. But with Osama Bin Laden still at large and Kim Jong-Il's nuclear arsenal looking ever more ominous, the war on terror was clearly far from over ...

How on earth was George W. Bush going to root his sinister bearded nemesis out of his cave, quell the escalating sectarian violence in Afganistan and deal with the growing threat of North Korea? By invading Iraq, of course.

For those who were just a little confused, Bush patiently spelled out the connection: 'The war on terror involves Saddam Hussein because of the nature of Saddam Hussein, the history of Saddam Hussein, and his willingness to terrorise himself.' But it wasn't merely this watertight logic that persuaded waverers of the urgent need to wage war in Iraq. Intelligence operatives provided Washington with absolutely incontrovertible vague rumours of Saddam's hidden stockpiles of Weapons of Mass Destruction. George W.'s staunch ally Tony Blair, too, was concerned that Iraqi missiles were just forty-five minutes away from British targets, and was in possession of the irrefutable hearsay to prove it. Saddam's stubborn refusal to give up these weapons led to the breakdown of diplomatic relations with the UN and made pre-emptive military action inevitable. France and Germany might have dragged their heels, but Bush and Blair stood firm: the only possible way to prevent a war with Iraq was by starting one.

'Operation Iraqi Freedom' was going to be a cakewalk. And so it was. After the initial 'shock and awe' air assault, Saddam's forces capitulated in double quick time, the Americans rolled into Baghdad and the Iraqi people were finally liberated from the yoke of tyranny. Except that some of them seemed a little fuzzy about the difference between 'liberation' and 'occupation'. Maybe they just hadn't heard Bush's 'State of the Union' address.

And where was their gratitude? After obligingly toppling a few statues of Saddam for CNN, the Iraqis then rather less obligingly split themselves up to pursue a complex and overlapping network of ethnic and religious campaigns of violence. Attacks on coalition troops came from Sunni 'insurgents' loyal to the old regime, but also from Shia militias who hated the old regime. Meanwhile, Sunni and Shia militias became locked in a bloody power struggle with each other and with the forces of the new Iraqi government, which is in turn broadly supported by the Kurds in the north, who are nevertheless also arming themselves just in case. Jeez, what's the matter with these people: can't they grasp the basics of the whole 'good versus evil' concept?

And that's not the only problem. The WMDs that made Saddam such a threat were so well hidden they don't seem to have shown up. There were all those embarrassing high jinks in Abu Ghraib prison, then more embarrassment when it turned out that Vice President Dick Cheney's old company, Halliburton, had not only been awarded contracts to reconstruct Iraq without having to compete, but had also accidentally overcharged the Pentagon for transporting oil to the gulf by sixty-one million dollars.

And then there's the death toll, of course. The number of coalition troops killed since the start of military action exceeds 3,000, and the number of Iraqi civilian casualties exceeds, oooh ... lots. Luckily no one seems to be keeping count. The ones that are still alive face death squads, suicide bombs, curfews, a crumbling infrastructure and lack of clean water and power. Those that can't adjust to the rigours of their new democratic lifestyle leave; 50,000 Iraqis flee the country every month, mostly to Syria and Jordan.

So military action might be failing to impose order, but those who think the Iraq war is an ill-conceived Vietnam-style quagmire and that the 'coalition of the willing' has run out of ideas are guilty yet again of misunderestimating George W. Luckily he has Plan B up his sleeve: yep, more military action.

Uday, Saddam's eldest son and a chip off the old block, used to jail the entire Iraq football team if their performance was below par.

One last 'surge' should sort things out for sure. In any case, those who criticise the war in Iraq are missing the point. WMDs or no, Saddam was a tyrant who simply had to be dealt with. And after all, who was in a better position to know just how much of a tyrant he really was than the very man responsible for overseeing Operation Iraqi Freedom, the now 'retired' US Secretary of Defence, Donald Rumsfeld? Rumsfeld got to know Saddam quite well in the eighties during those arms-dealing trips to Baghdad, when Saddam was using chemical weapons not only against his neighbours in Iran, but against his own Kurdish ethnic minorities.

Uday also kept a collection of lions and tigers in cages at his palace.

Saddam erected a new statue of himself every year on his birthday.

President of Iraq since 1979, Saddam was ostensibly part of the Ba'ath or 'renaissance' Party, but his own authority was total and often brutally exercised. And when it came to power, he certainly believed in keeping it in the family. By marrying his first cousin and promoting his extensive network of brothers and cousins to government positions, he created a ruling dynasty with himself at the centre.

Just as in any loving and close-knit family, though, there was always the danger of the occasional tiff. Saddam had his two sons-in-law (who were also his cousins) killed for disloyalty, and arranged a fatal 'accident' for his wife's brother. His eldest son, Uday, shot Saddam's brother, while Saddam in turn would have executed Uday, had it not been for the intervention of King Hussein of Jordan. Saddam's execution may have rid the world of a brutal despot with a terrible human rights record, but it also eliminated Kim Jong-Il's only serious rival for the title of the world's most unhinged dictator. Saddam's extravagant lifestyle and bizarre habits were easily a match for the North Korean Elvis-impersonator. When US forces took possession of his twenty-plus palaces, for instance, they discovered gold-leaf thrones, private casinos and underground runways for Saddam's private jets. He may have enjoyed shooting guns in the air and going fishing with grenades, but the Butcher of Baghdad was also clearly a man who enjoyed more cultural pursuits, keeping a library stocked entirely with the writings of Joseph Stalin and building the Saddam Art Center: a museum with nothing but paintings of himself.

Saddam was the Imelda Marcos of hats.
He had a huge collection of hats, including bulletproof ones.

He was quite particular when it came to etiquette, requiring visitors to have their clothes washed, sterilised and even x-rayed before granting them an audience. They also had to greet him with a kiss near each armpit, an act which wouldn't be near the top of anyone's wish-list, but which was not as unpleasant as it sounds: obsessive to the point of neurosis about personal hygiene, Saddam advocated washing twice a day and gave detailed instructions about the behaviour of his subjects. 'It is not appropriate for someone to attend a gathering or to be with his children with his body odour trailing behind emitting a sweet or stinky smell mixed with perspiration.' Men should bathe at least once a day, he declared, but women definitely needed two baths, since females are 'more delicate, and the smell of a woman is more noticeable'.

Iraq's national newspaper had to carry a different picture of Saddam on the front page every day.

The Iraqi leader's approach to food was equally particular. Ever security-conscious, he had three meals a day prepared at each of his many palaces in order to fool potential assassins as to his whereabouts. He also employed the services of a food taster. That is, until the unusually sadistic Uday clubbed the taster to death for some minor indiscretion. (Kids! What can you do?)

Saddam liked meat, and plenty of it. Guests attending one of Saddam's famously opulent poolside barbecues could expect copious quantities of steak and chicken. (Or death, depending on how the host felt about them. The chemical thallium was routinely used by Saddam to fatally poison the food of his enemies.) And the Butcher of Baghdad's favourite kind of meat? Gazelle, naturally. Specially reared on a farm outside Baghdad, they were fed a diet of cardamom for several weeks before Saddam hand-picked one for his plate.

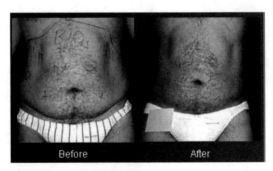

Saddam was worried about his weight, and once tried to import a liposuction machine to Baghdad.

Life wasn't just one long barbecue for Saddam, though. The soul, too, needed nourishment. 'If we were satisfied by food, we would be transformed into worms or poultry,' he reminded his people, and such words must have been a comfort as shortages caused by the US embargo kicked in, and a combination of starvation and disease claimed a reported three million Iraqi children.

Equally inspirational must have been Saddam's pious example. One of his unfinished projects was the construction of the world's largest mosque. Taller than the Eiffel Tower, it was to be surrounded by an ornamental lake the size of seventy football pitches, the creation of which involved the River Tigris being rerouted.

Once his regime had crumbled and he had gone into hiding, Saddam had to put up with the slightly less grandiose surroundings of a hole in the ground. And there was no more barbecued gazelle on the menu when he was discovered and held in US custody. But Saddam was quick to adapt to his new surroundings, and cultivated less elaborate tastes. Apparently keen on Doritos corn chips, he would single-handedly demolish a family-sized bag in ten minutes. And in an irony that surely even George Bush would grasp, the former scourge of America then spent his last days eating hamburgers and fries.

Makhlama (spicy spinach omelette)

Directions

Chop the onion and chilli pepper, and fry in oil with the cumin and turmeric. When the onion softens, add the spinach and the other greens, finely chopped, and allow them to cook for a few minutes. Add the beaten eggs, cover the pan and leave until the omelette is set. Turn it over and cook the other side.

Now make another twenty for each of your presidential palaces.

You will need

a largish bunch of fresh spinach, chopped
6 eggs
1 onion
1 small hot chilli pepper
a handful of chopped parsley
a handful of chopped dill
1 teaspoon turmeric
1 teaspoon cumin

Pomegranate Soup

You will need

¼ lb minced beef
1 small green chilli pepper
a handful of breadcrumbs
1 teaspoon cumin
1 teaspoon tarragon
1 teaspoon cayenne pepper
a handful of chopped coriander
a handful of chopped mint
2 cloves of garlic
3 tablespoons pomegranate concentrate

Directions

Make the meatballs by mixing the beef, chopped onion, breadcrumbs, cumin and cayenne and forming into small balls. Fry the meatballs in the oil, turning them until they brown evenly. Chop and stir in the coriander, chilli and garlic. After about 5 minutes, add remaining ingredients and about a pint of stock (vegetable or beef). Bring to the boil, then cover the saucepan and simmer over medium heat for about 40 minutes. Serve.

Yoghurt Soup

A recipe so simple even the most intellectually-challenged of world leaders could manage it.

Directions

Boil the rice for 25 minutes in about half a pint of water. Reduce the heat and stir in the yoghurt and crushed garlic, as well as a pinch of salt and pepper. Heat it up again, stirring constantly, but don't let it come to the boil. Add the mint and serve.

Mnazellah

This is a kind of Iraqi goulash. Serve with bread. Or chips. Or anything you like, really.

You will need

½ lb flour
3 aubergines
1 onion
1 can chickpeas
3 cloves of garlic
1 hot chilli pepper
4 ripe tomatoes, diced
1 teaspoon nutmeg
1 teaspoon coriander
a sprinkling of fresh parsley and mint

Directions

Chop the onion, chilli pepper and garlic and sauté them in oil. Add the aubergine, cubed, and cook over medium heat for a few minutes, stirring regularly to avoid any sticking. When it starts to brown, add the tomatoes and spices, cover, and cook for a few minutes. Next chuck in the drained chickpeas, and cook for about 20 minutes. Stir in the fresh herbs, season and allow to cook for another 5 minutes before serving.

Tongue of the Judge

This doesn't really involve a judge's tongue. That would be disgusting and probably illegal.

Directions

First make the sauce: sauté one chopped onion, add the tomatoes, tomato purée and turmeric. Add a mugful of water, season and simmer for 20 minutes or so. Now chop the stalk and bottom from the aubergines and then cut them lengthwise into slices about a quarter of an inch thick. Fry the slices quickly in hot oil so they're browned but not too soggy. Set them aside and make the stuffing by mixing the minced meat and the other chopped onion. Season it and form into little sausages. Roll each of the sausages up in an aubergine slice and lay them on a baking dish. Pour over the tomato sauce and stick the dish in a medium hot oven for 40 minutes, or until the sauce is bubbling.

You will need

2 large aubergines
1 lb minced lamb or beef
2 onions
2 tomatoes, chopped
3 tablespoons tomato purée
1 teaspoon turmeric

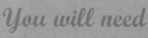

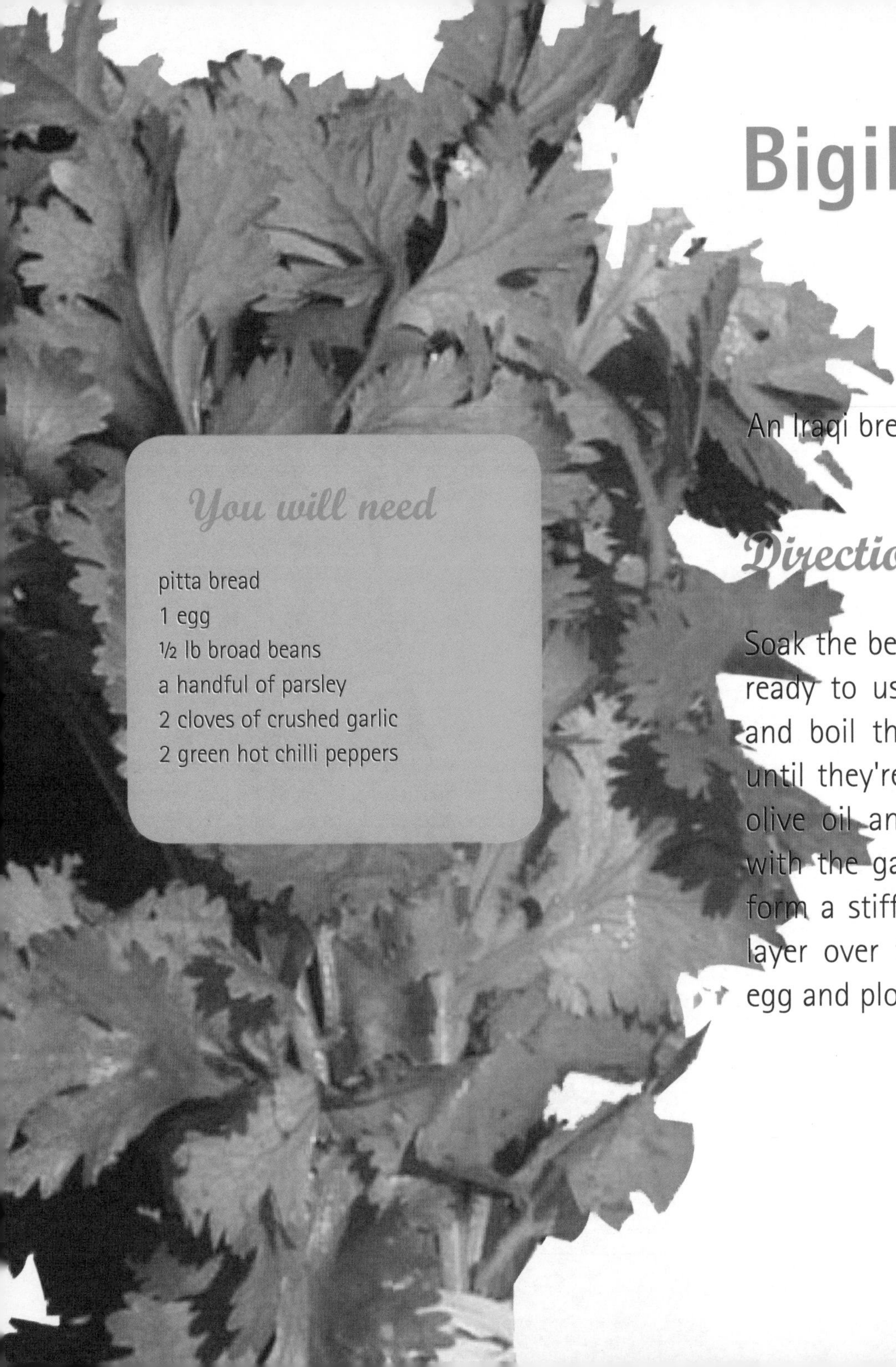

Bigilla

An Iraqi breakfast recipe.

Directions

Soak the beans overnight. When you're ready to use them, change the water and boil them for about 40 minutes, until they're soft. Add a tablespoon of olive oil and mash it all up together with the garlic, pepper and parsley to form a stiff paste. Spread it in a thick layer over the pitta bread, poach the egg and plonk it on top.

You will need

pitta bread
1 egg
½ lb broad beans
a handful of parsley
2 cloves of crushed garlic
2 green hot chilli peppers

Iraqi Pink Rice

Directions

Sauté the chopped onion in oil for a couple of minutes, then add the rice, uncooked, and stir well. Next, stir in the tomato purée and then add the right amount of water. Add the cumin, season generously and cover the pan. Leave it over a low heat for 20 minutes and then remove it from the heat, still covered, and let it sit for a minute or two. On removing the lid you should have beautiful pink rice.

You will need

Basmati rice (measure it out using a cup; for two cups of rice you need to add three cups of water)

1 onion

1 teaspoon cumin

1 tablespoon tomato purée

Aubergine and Yoghurt

This is a starter or side dish, usually served with pitta bread.

You will need

1 large aubergine
3 tablespoons thick plain yoghurt
3 cloves of garlic, crushed
a squirt of lemon juice

Directions

Cut the top and bottom off the aubergine and slice it lengthwise into slices half an inch thick. Fry the slices in hot oil, browning them on each side. Drain them on a paper towel then arrange in layers on a serving dish. Mix the garlic, lemon juice and yoghurt together and pour over the aubergines. Sprinkle with a little salt and serve.

Cardamom Cookies (hadgi bdah)

If you have any cardamom left over from feeding it to your gazelles, why not make these tasty cookies?

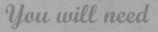

You will need

½ lb flour
1 teaspoon ground cardamom
a pinch of salt
a medium smidgen of baking powder
½ lb sugar
4 eggs
½ lb ground almonds
oodles of whole almonds

Directions

Preheat the oven to 350°F (175°C) and grease some baking sheets. Sift the flour with the cardamom, salt and baking powder. Then beat the eggs with the sugar until creamy. Stir in the flour mixture followed by the ground almonds. Form the dough into small balls (moisten your hands first), then place on a baking sheet and flatten by pressing a whole almond into the centre. Bake for just over 10 minutes or until they start to brown, then turn out onto a wire rack and NO, YOU CAN'T HAVE ONE YET! Wait until they're cool!

Um Ali

You will need

10 oz cooked puff pastry
2 tablespoons lemon juice
1 egg, beaten
a pinch of cinnamon
½ pint single cream
½ pint milk
½ lb sugar
a generous handful of chopped pistachio nuts
same quantity of flaked almonds

Quite probably named in honour of 'Chemical Ali', Saddam's infamously untrustworthy information minister, this is another Iraqi dessert.

Directions

Grease a glass baking dish and preheat a hot oven. Crumble the puff pastry into the dish and mix with the nuts and lemon juice. Heat the milk with the sugar and cinnamon to almost boiling, before slowly adding the beaten egg. Pour this over the stuff in the dish. Top with the cream and bake for about half an hour until it starts to brown. Prepare for a cardiac arrest.

Iran

With a recorded history stretching back several millennia, Iran, formerly known as Persia, is currently the longest-lasting continuous civilisation in existence ...

But not for much longer, perhaps. As the war of words between Tehran and Washington hots up, it seems as though George W. has it firmly in his sights, and it may be next in line for some good old-fashioned regime change; and, of course, some thorough rebuilding. And if Iraq is anything to go by, there might not be much left of Iran's ancient civilisation except a pile of rubble once Uncle Sam has finished rebuilding it.

But this is no time to be worrying about a few old monuments. Iran's nuclear programme is gathering pace and recently-elected President Ahmadinejad, the newest tyrant in the Axis of Evil, says there's 'no brake and no reverse'. Sounds like he's a highly dangerous maniac who shouldn't be in charge of a medium-sized family hatchback, let alone a large nation with nuclear capability. And what about the 10,000 square metres of underground halls and tunnels he's reputedly building? Are they yet more hidden nuclear facilities, or perhaps a top-secret Bond-villain-style subterranean base? Either way, it's got EVIL written all over it. Tehran has already broken the terms of the nuclear non-proliferation treaty, and if that weren't bad enough, there are unconfirmed 'intelligence' reports suggesting that chief evildoer Kim Jong-Il has been sharing some of his bomb-making secrets with the Iranians.

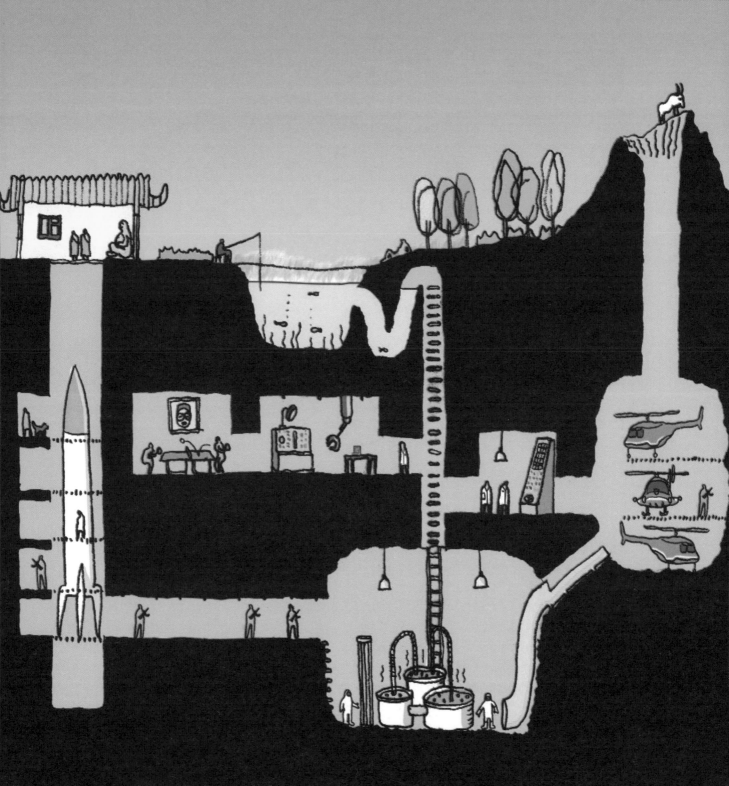

With the situation in the Middle East a veritable powder keg, only a madman would want an aggressive and unpredictable nation getting its hands on nuclear weapons. Unless that nation is Israel, of course, in which case it's OK because they're not pointing them at us. Anyway, the plain fact is that Iran needs to be stopped, and stopped now. It's a repressive and undemocratic regime whose downtrodden citizens are just crying out to be liberated by their friends in America. And no wonder: now that they've seen their neighbours in Iraq enjoying the benefits of liberation they must be anxious for some of the same. Every time you watch the news they always seem to be out in the street voicing their support of the US. Or at least that's how White House experts are interpreting it. And anyway, why else would the poor oppressed Iranians be waving those US flags around? Just a shame they have to keep setting fire to them ... still, it must be cold in Tehran this time of year.

President Ahmadinejad is probably the only evil tyrant to hold a PhD in Transport Engineering.

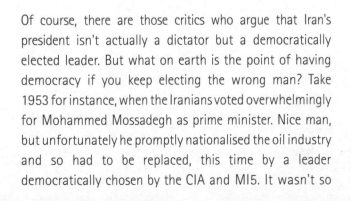

Of course, there are those critics who argue that Iran's president isn't actually a dictator but a democratically elected leader. But what on earth is the point of having democracy if you keep electing the wrong man? Take 1953 for instance, when the Iranians voted overwhelmingly for Mohammed Mossadegh as prime minister. Nice man, but unfortunately he promptly nationalised the oil industry and so had to be replaced, this time by a leader democratically chosen by the CIA and MI5. It wasn't so much an election, more of a military coup, but at least the new leader, the Shah of Persia, was far more sensible when it came to Western economic interests. The Shah then held power until 1979 when the Iranians, who just never seem to know what's good for them, ousted him in a popular revolution and the exiled religious leader Ayatollah Khomeini was swept to power, establishing Iran as an Islamic state.

ABSTAIN FROM
HOLDING MEETINGS,
FROM BLATHERING,
FROM PUBLISHING
PROTESTS.
OTHERWISE I
WILL BREAK YOUR
TEETH.

A.K.

Infamous for outlawing all forms of enjoyment and never smiling even once during his entire rule, the Ayatollah's attitude to the US was made clear during the first days of his government when the American embassy was occupied and hostages held for a rather embarrassing 444 days before finally being released. After a terrible start, Khomeini's relations with the US continued in more or less the same vein, and his regime was blacklisted. He had a record of human rights abuses as long as your arm, and an approach to political dialogue that was a tad on the robust side. 'Abstain from holding meetings, from blathering, from publishing protests. Otherwise I will break your teeth,' the Ayatollah informed his opponents. He also found time for a spot of literary appreciation in his spare time, famously issuing a fatwa or death sentence on British author Salman Rushdie, after taking a dislike to his novel *The Satanic Verses*.

In sum, Khomeini was considered a nasty piece of work in Washington, particularly once he started declaring his support for such bloodthirsty terrorists as Yasser Arafat and, er, Nelson Mandela. At the same time though, those in the 1980s' Reagan administration never seriously entertained plans to topple the Ayatollah. And why would they? For a start, Iran was far too occupied fighting someone else to be a real threat: its bloody eight-year war with Saddam's Iraq cost over half a million Iranian lives. Oh, and also Washington was making rather a lot of money selling arms to both sides. There was yet more embarrassment in the White House when it was revealed that, despite publicly backing Saddam, American agents were also secretly selling anti-tank missiles to Iran and funding the South American Contras with the proceeds.

After Khomeini's death it seemed as though Iran was becoming less hostile to the West. The reformist president Khatami relaxed some of the more unsavoury aspects of Iranian law involving beheadings and amputations, and encouraged greater democracy and freedom of speech. He also made encouragingly pro-Western noises, appearing on CNN advocating a 'dialogue of civilisations' between the Arab world and the West. And in the immediate aftermath of 9/11 Iran extended a helping hand to America during its campaign against the Taliban in Afghanistan, supporting the US-backed Northern Alliance and assisting in the selection and nomination of pro-US Afghan president Karzai.

Two thirds of the population are under thirty), and Clearasil is one of the county's biggest imports.

One food Ahmadinejad definitely doesn't like is burgers. As hardline Mayor of Tehran he closed down all the fast food restaurants.

Given this thawing of relations between the two countries, there were those who were pretty surprised when Iran was named as one of the key members of the Axis of Evil, not least the Iranians themselves. Surely Iran was making strides towards the kind of democratic reform America advocated, as well as aiding it in the war on terror? Not a bit of it. All this friendliness was clearly just a mask for evil. Luckily, Bush is nobody's fool, and wasn't taken in for a minute by this apparent greater cooperation with the US. And ever since exposing Iran as a hotbed of evilness, he's been turning up the heat, warning the Iranians in no uncertain terms to stop their terror-sponsoring ways and turn off those nuclear plants, or else.

Critics argue that US intransigence is backing Iran into a corner, playing into the hands of anti-American elements like the ultra-conservative Mr Ahmadinejad and making impossible the kinds of democratic reform that Washington says it wants. Certainly Ahmadinejad has been more than living up to his reputation in recent months. He might be new to all this, but he's been coming out with the kinds of things any seasoned dangerous tyrant would be envious of.

And while he eschews religious robes in favour of the casual look, his statements are purest evil. He managed to horrify both political liberals and fashion pundits alike when he appeared on CNN wearing a beige anorak, suggesting that Israel should be wiped off the map, and that the Holocaust did not take place. He also refused to condemn Hezbollah, which is proof enough to the hawks in Washington that he's a supporter of terrorism. They're arguing that he's supplying the insurgent militia in Iraq with arms. Factual evidence of this is difficult to find, but then Bush isn't one to let evidence muddy the issue.

Axis of Elvis

x

In any case, Iran must remain a danger while it's in the grip of religious fundamentalism. Or at least that's the considered opinion of many of the fundamentalist Christians advising Bush on policy matters. What we need to do is replace those stony-faced religious clerics with leaders who are a bit more cuddly. Possibly ones who look a bit less ... Islamic. And certainly some with less facial hair since, as everyone knows, beards are usually a sign of evil (just look at Castro). All in all, things are looking black for Mr Ahmadinejad; what with his unfortunate refusal to recognise Israel, his nuclear ambitions, and not forgetting that enormous oil supply he's sitting on, regime change is only a matter of time. Bush has declared he has 'no plans to invade Iran'. But then again, having no plans didn't stop him when it came to war in Iraq: he much prefers to play things by ear. And, let's face it, all those troops are over in Iraq already. Isn't Iran on the way home?

Iranians are blog-crazy. Blogging is more popular there than almost anywhere else in the world.

But forget about imminent world war: the burning question is, of course, what does the new biggest threat to the Western world like to eat? Well, President Ahmadinejad is a simple man from a poor background (his father was a blacksmith), so as you might expect, he likes uncomplicated and traditional fare. Apparently he's partial to koresht, a plain dish of rice and stew. No surprises there, then, but what of his dour predecessor, the late Ayatollah Khomeini? Could it be true, as intelligence reports suggest, that his favourite food was a McDonald's Happy Meal?

Iranian women form a two-thirds majority of university students, and can be found in the police force and fire service.

Gormeh Sabzi

You will need

1 onion, chopped
1 teaspoon turmeric
the juice of 1 lemon
½ can of red kidney beans
1 large potato, diced
3 or 4 spring onions
a bunch of fresh spinach
a quantity of parsley
a handful of fresh coriander
a cluster of chives
a batch of fresh green fenugreek
meat, if you're that way inclined. Lamb is ideal, cut into cubes, although you can make this stew without it.

This is a bean and herb casserole (sabzi means 'herb'). It's a staple of the Persian diet and the key to making it is to find yourself some fenugreek. Yes, it's a herb. Don't cheat by using whatever green stuff you can find in your kitchen!

Directions

Fry the onion until golden, adding the turmeric. Throw in the meat if you're using it and turn the heat up, stirring until it browns slightly. Cover with water and add the drained kidney beans and season with salt and pepper. Cover with a lid and simmer it for about an hour until the meat is tender (if you're making it without, half an hour will do). Take a different pan and fry the potato until it starts to brown, then add it to the stew and simmer for a further 15 minutes.

Meanwhile, finely chop and sauté all the greens in the pan you just used for the potatoes. When they begin to wilt, add them to the stew along with the lemon juice and simmer for 15 minutes more, stirring and adding more liquid if it sticks to the pan. Serve it up with white rice.

Tongue with Mushrooms

Ah, the perennial problem of leftover cows' tongues clogging up your kitchen cupboards. Annoying, isn't it? Never mind, here's something you can do with them.

Directions

Wash the meat and boil, removing any scum that forms on the water's surface. Add the garlic, onions and herbs, stick in a bit of salt and pepper and simmer for 4 to 5 hours (seriously, haven't you got better things to do?), topping up water as necessary. You should be left with about a cup's worth of liquid at the end. Remove the tongue, peel off skin, allow to cool and then slice thinly. Fry the mushrooms in butter, add tomato pureé and tongue stock, and bring to the boil. Pour sauce over the tongue and serve with rice.

You will need

1 beef tongue (or 2 sheep tongues. Whatever you do, don't use cat tongues; there's never enough to go round)
2 or 3 cloves of garlic, sliced thinly
2 onions, sliced thinly
dollop of tomato purée
2 good handfuls of mushrooms
butter
fresh parsley, coriander, dill and spring onions (chopped)

Donbalaan (sheep testicles)

You will need

4 sheep testicles (if you don't have any actual animal genitalia to hand, then use balls of sausage meat and your imagination)
2 eggs
breadcrumbs
chopped parsley

Not feeling queasy after handling cow's tongue? Then how about some sheep testicle?

Directions

Clean the testicles, cut in two and remove the skin. Sprinkle with salt and pepper. Put the eggs in a bowl, mix and season. Next dip your testicles in the egg and then in the breadcrumbs. Shallow fry until golden brown and sprinkle with parsley.

Adas Polow
(rice with dates and lentils)

Directions

Wash the rice and then soak it in cold water for an hour. Boil the lentils until they're cooked but not too soft, then drain. Slice the onion and fry til it starts to brown. Sprinkle half half the saffron and the cumin over the onions, then add the dates, frying for a few more minutes before adding the raisins and the cooked lentils. Drain the rice and put it in a pan of boiling water. After about 5 minutes it should be done, but still slightly firm. Rinse and drain it once again.

In a large pan heat some oil and add a cupful of water to it. When the two are boiling together, sprinkle in the rest of the saffron and then start to ladle in the rice, making an even layer. Follow this with a layer of lentils and dates, and carry on until you've used up all the ingredients. The final layer should be rice, and you need to make the layers thicker in the middle than at the edges to create a kind of dome shape. Now make a few holes in the mixture all the way to the bottom of the pan. Cover and leave to cook for a few minutes until the rice begins to steam. Then reduce the heat to minimum, add a few tablespoons of extra water and oil, and cover the pan with a lid wrapped in a clean tea towel. Leave it alone for about 50 minutes. When it's done, let it cool for a short while, then remove the lid and place a large plate upside down on top of the pan. Turn the whole lot over so that the mixture comes out onto the plate. Now eat it!

Rice and dates. Sounds an unlikely combination, but it's extremely tasty.

You will need

1 large onion
some Basmati rice (roughly a handful for each person you're feeding)
green lentils (half the quantity of the rice)
pitted dates (How many do you think Iran's anorak-wearing President Amedinejad would use? Well, that's how many you need.)
raisins
1 teaspoon saffron
1 teaspoon cumin

Koresht Fesenjan (chicken casserole)

You will need

1 lb chicken pieces
½ lb ground walnuts
3 onions, chopped
4 mugfuls pomegranate juice
2 tablespoons sugar
pinch of cardamom
1 teaspoon salt

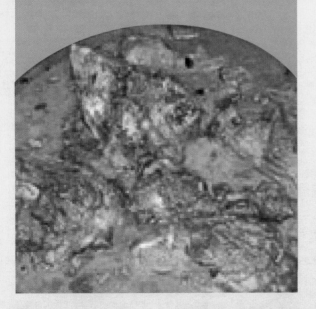

Khoresht is a delicately spiced Iranian casserole or stew, usually served with rice.

Directions

Sauté the chicken and onion in oil for about 15 minutes, stirring so it doesn't stick to the pan. Now chuck in the other ingredients, reduce the heat and cover the pan. Simmer gently for 2 hours, stirring occasionally. The sauce should be thick and aromatic, but you may need to add more water while it's cooking if it gets too stodgy.

Koresht Gaimeh (split-pea and potato casserole)

You will need

3 tablespoons tomato purée
3 onions, sliced
1 lb potatoes, chopped fairly small
juice of 1 lime
½ lb lamb or beef, cubed
½ lb dried split peas
1 teaspoon paprika
1 teaspoon turmeric

You can use meat if you're feeling carnivorous, but it's not essential.

Directions

Bring the split peas to the boil, then set them aside to soak for 2 hours. Sauté the onions and the meat for about 10 minutes, then add the tomato purée and spices and give it a good stir. Add a little water and simmer until the meat is tender. Now drain the split peas and add them, along with the potatoes, to the pan. Add enough water to cover the potatoes and continue to simmer for about 40 minutes or until the stew is thick and the potatoes soft. Squeeze in the lime juice at the end, and cook for another few minutes. Serve it up with rice.

Kofte

Kofte (sometimes called kufte or kafteh) are a kind of meatball found in Iran and many other parts of the Middle East. They're often served in a tomato sauce or yoghurt, but you can eat them any way you like.

You will need

1 lb minced beef
handful of chopped parsley
1 onion, finely chopped
salt and pepper to taste

Directions

Put all the ingredients in a bowl and mash them all together with your hands. Form into golf-ball-sized patties and fry, grill or barbecue until slightly browned. Save the ones you don't eat; you can play golf with them.

Kuku (Persian omelette)

This Persian omelette has lots of green things in it. They're good for you!

Directions

Chop all the green stuff finely, then mix it in a bowl with the beaten eggs, spices and seasoning. Shallow fry the mixture in oil in a non-stick pan over a medium heat until it browns slightly, then flip it over and do the other side. Serve with pitta bread. Chew. Swallow. Repeat.

You will need

2 eggs
1 leek
salt and pepper
1 teaspoon cumin
a generous handful of each of the following:
parsley
spinach
spring onions
coriander

Halva

3 oz flour
3 oz sugar
3 tablespoons rose water
1 teaspoon saffron
chopped pistachios and almonds

This dense, sweet dessert is found in various different forms across the Middle East.

Directions

Add the flour into a frying pan of hot oil and stir until thick and golden. Remove it from the heat. Dissolve the sugar in a glass of water and then boil the mixture in a pan, along with the saffron and rose water. Add the cooled flour to the sugar syrup and mix well. The consistency should be fairly thick. Sprinkle with nuts before serving.

Zulbia

You will need

For the batter:
4 tablespoons water
4 oz flour
2 eggs
2 tablespoons butter
squirt of lemon juice

For the syrup:
4 oz sugar
juice of half a lemon
4 tablespoons water
1 teaspoon cardamom

For evil-doers with a sweet tooth, these traditional Persian desserts are perfect. Zulbia is often served along with bamiah - similar fried-batter sweets made in little ridged ball shapes resembling lady's fingers or okra ('bamiah' is Persian for 'okra').

Directions

Make the syrup first, by heating the ingredients together in a pan, stirring constantly until the mixture thickens. Remove it from the heat, and then prepare the batter. Heat the water, butter and lemon juice in a pan, then whisk in the flour, making sure it doesn't get lumpy. Now whisk in the eggs too, until the batter is smooth. Heat about half an inch of oil in a frying pan and then, using a cake icer, pipe the batter in spiral shapes into the oil. When the spirals are slightly crispy, remove them and dunk them straight into the syrup until they're coated. Put them somewhere to cool, then serve them up.

North Korea

A distinct lack of either beards or oil made North Korea the wild card in the original three Axis of Evil countries ...

The fact that it was a hotbed of international terrorism and an ally of Iraq and Iran came as a bit of a surprise, probably not least to North Korea itself, which exists in a state of near total isolation from the rest of the world. However, since then the country has been doing its best to live up to its evil reputation, pulling out of a nuclear profileration agreement, kicking out UN weapons inspectors and generally doing the things rogue states are expected to do.

In 2006 it upped the ante, test firing long-range Taepodong-2 missiles over the Sea of Japan. And then there was the little matter of a controlled nuclear explosion carried out just three months later. But, while it may be evil, it's hard to tell just how evil: the hermit kingdom of North Korea is something of a mystery. Comparatively little is known about day-to-day life there, since foreigners are allowed to visit only under the watchful gaze of a government-appointed guide. Entry rules have been relaxed slightly in recent years to accommodate more adventurous tourists, but these are confined to strictly designated areas.

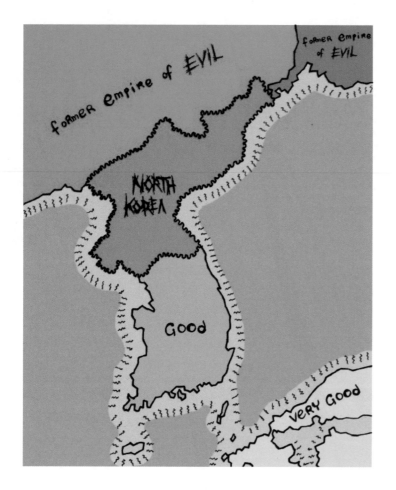

Established in 1948, the Democratic People's Republic of Korea was the result of a post-war partition of the Korean peninsula that was initially intended only as a temporary measure. While US troops occupied the south, a Soviet-backed government was installed in the north, led by the Red Army-trained general Kim Il-Sung. As cold war hostilities became more entrenched, so did the border between the two Koreas, and Kim Il-Sung became the hugely influential architect of the fledgling state.

He still retains the title of president, although now takes something of a back seat in policy decisions, as he died more than ten years ago. On his death in 1994, the reins of power passed to the man best qualified to take over the demanding job of dictator. This turned out to be Kim's son, Kim Jong-Il.

Kim Jong-Il is said to be a big
fan of the films Rambo and
Friday the Thirteenth.

Despite its initial close ties with the USSR, North Korea has gradually distanced itself from Soviet-style communism and embraced the principle of Juche. Sometimes translated as 'self-reliance', Juche is a peculiar mixture of Western Marxism and Eastern Confucianism which stresses the importance of a unified, indigenous Korean culture, and encourages its autonomous development well away from contaminating foreign influences. This insular philosophy explains both North Korea's isolationist stance, and its reasons for wanting reunification with its capitalist neighbour to the south.

However, while the Juche ideology of national and cultural unity is ideal for citizens wanting to participate in mass displays of folk dancing, it tends to be less beneficial for those wanting to express their individuality or criticise the government. Dissent is not tolerated in North Korea and it has one of the worst human rights records in the world: There are reputedly 150,000 political prisoners in detention camps, although these figures are hard to verify, as are the conditions in which prisoners are

STEP I

STEP II

STEP III

In a highly regimented society, party control extends to most areas of everyday life, and radio and TV sets come pre-tuned to government channels, allowing North Koreans to enjoy such programmes as 'Let Us Trim Our Hair in Accordance with Socialist Lifestyle', which gives valuable warnings about the dangers of long and untidy hair. Not only does excessive hair betray an unpatriotic attitude, it may also prevent valuable oxygen from getting to the brain. No advice is given to women about hair length (possibly their brains don't require as much oxygen) but the programme sensibly advises North Korean men that their hair should be no more than five inches on top. However, a generous seven inches are permitted for balding men wishing to disguise their thinning hair with a comb-over, Donald Trump-style.

Whether or not Kim Jong-Il's distinctive bouffant hairdo conforms to this ruling is not known. The reclusive 'beloved leader' - who has been heard to speak publicly just once - is as much of an enigma as his country. Is this reticence merely modesty on the part of a remarkable man who once composed six operas in two years, scored eleven holes in one during his first round of golf, and is responsible for designing the enormous Juche Tower in the state capital, Pyongyang? Well, yes, if you believe the government-controlled media. But however outlandish these claims, it seems as though the reality behind the personality cult is even more bizarre.

"I KNOW IT'S THE BREAST STROKE, BUT I WANT YOU TO HOLD ME **UNDER THE CHIN**"

A chubby and unprepossessing figure sporting his trademark Mao suit, outsize sunglasses and platform heels to boost his 5'2" stature, Kim might not look much of a playboy, but after a hard day as a ruthless tyrant he apparently likes nothing better than relaxing in the company of his private 'pleasure brigade' of women, or doing a few laps of his swimming pool on a special motorised float, under the watchful gaze of his nubile nurses.

Or alternatively he might retreat to his private cinema to enjoy one of his 20,000 videos. He is, apparently, especially fond of James Bond films, and in 1978 demonstrated his passion for cinema by kidnapping the South Korean director Shin Sang-Ok and his actress wife. The couple then spent several years as Kim's 'guests', making films to his instructions, including a socialist version of 'Godzilla'.

But Kim is even more serious about his other big passion: food. Clearly a man for whom only the best is good enough, Kim employs a team of women to check his rice, grain by grain, discarding any that are not uniform in size and colour. And when eating pizza, he reportedly demands that the distance between each olive has to be carefully measured to ensure even distribution. Kim has a taste for the exotic too, enjoying a spot of roast donkey, and flying in chefs from Japan to prepare sashimi, or live fish.

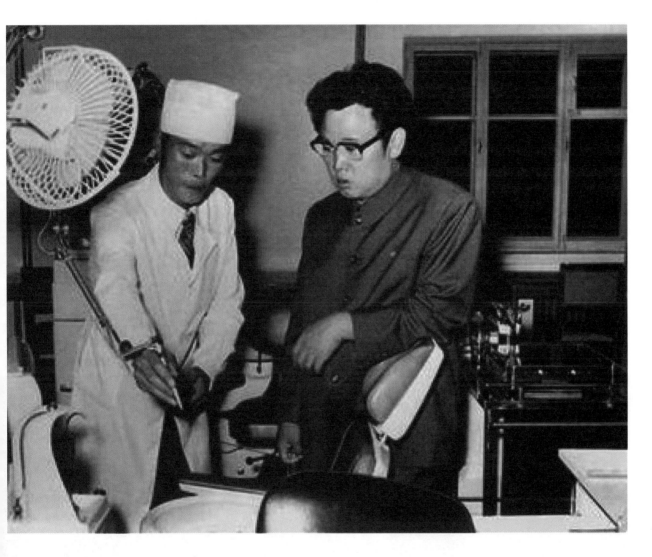

He spares no expense in acquiring only the finest in world cuisine, spending over half a million dollars per year on top-of-the-range Hennessy cognac, and importing such rare delicacies as camels' feet, lion extract from Tanzania, blue shark liver from Angola and live lobster from France. And while it may be a one-party state, Kim is determined to make it a party to remember; his banquets are reported to last up to four days. But in case this kind of excess should cause him to pile on the pounds, Kim has established the Long Life Research Institute in Pyongyang, which employs a staff of 200 doctors, all dedicated to optimising his nutritional health and ensuring his rich diet does not affect the beloved leader's health.

Luckily, for Kim's subjects the perils of overindulgence are less of a worry. The party machinery may be good at overseeing propaganda, but it has proved less adept at controlling the state agricultural industry, where under-investment and mismanagement are rife and have sometimes led to chronic food shortages. In the early 1990s, exacerbated by the drying up of food aid from Eastern Bloc allies, these shortages developed into full-scale famine in which as many as two million people (ten per cent of the population) may have died. Many survived only by living on grass and weeds ground into flour and made into a basic form of noodle.

The situation may have improved, but it's far from stable. The only thing standing between North Korea and yet more famine is the food supplied by neighbouring China, an arrangement which is now looking tenuous. The Beijing government, none too impressed with Kim's recent nuclear tests, has been making ominous noises in the direction of Pyongyang.

In 1950 North Korea invaded its neighbour to the south, sparking the Korean War.

North Korea has one of the largest standing armies in the world: one in twenty of the population is in the army.

China is also one of the few places where North Korean food is enjoyed. Several state-sponsored North Korean restaurants have opened there, and it's an increasingly chic choice among Chinese foodies. Few people in the West may have sampled North Korean cuisine, but everyone's heard of dog stew. This highly controversial (and highly unappetising) dish is Korea's most infamous contribution to the world of food. The idea of marinating your pooch in a low to moderate oven may be anathema to Western animal lovers, but for many Koreans, north and south of the border, it's not only a delicacy but a tastier version of Viagra. Opposition to the cruelties of the dog meat trade remains relatively small in scale and is unlikely to diminish the dish's popularity in Korea because of its reputed benefits in terms of health and virility.

Kim Jong-Il has a wine cellar consisting of 10,000 bottles.

According to the North Korean media, Kim Jong-Il's birth was marked by a double rainbow in the sky and the appearance of a new star.

Dog Stew

Dog stew remains popular in both North and South Korea despite protests by Westerners and an increasingly vocal animal rights lobby. Its continued appeal lies at least partly in the fact that dog meat is believed to have medicinal properties, enhancing the stamina and vitality of those who eat it; for Koreans, Dog Stew is a form of Viagra.

NB. It can be quite difficult to persuade Fido to sit still in the cooking pot, so for vegetarians and those who are just too busy to cook a whole dog, Quorn pieces make an acceptable substitute.

You will need

1 medium-sized dog, boiled until tender (at least 1 hour - dog is quite tough. But if you're using Quorn, skip this stage) spinach, Chinese cabbage and other assorted greens
gojuchang

Directions

Place the cabbage, spinach etc., in the bottom of a cooking pot. Place the dog meat or Quorn pieces over the greens and spread some gojuchang (Korean spicy red pepper paste) on top. Now cover with stock (either dog or vegetable stock) and simmer for half an hour until it looks cooked.

Before

Bibimbap

You will need

2 small carrots
1 large courgette
a medium-sized fistful of beansprouts
a similar quantity of mushrooms
2 eggs
1 mugful of rice (jasmine or plain)

Bibim is a Korean word meaning 'stir together', for reasons that become apparent once this dish is served. There are innumerable variants of this simple recipe and it can be adapted to include many different ingredients. Dolsot Bibimbap is a variation that involves serving the dish in a heated dolsot or stone bowl, so that the rice at the bottom of the dish is crunchy.

Directions

Cook the rice and split between two bowls. Cut the carrots and courgette into thin strips and sauté them in oil, add the chopped mushrooms and then, shortly afterwards, the beansprouts. Arrange the vegetables on top of the rice. Then gently fry the eggs until cooked but soft in the middle. Place one in each bowl, on top of the vegetables. Koreans usually add a little red pepper paste, known as gojuchang, but if you can't find any then use chilli pepper paste, soy sauce or sesame oil.

OK, so you've prepared a beautiful-looking Bibimbap. Now get ready to stir everything together into a disgusting mush before eating, just as the North Koreans do. On your marks, get set ... bibim!

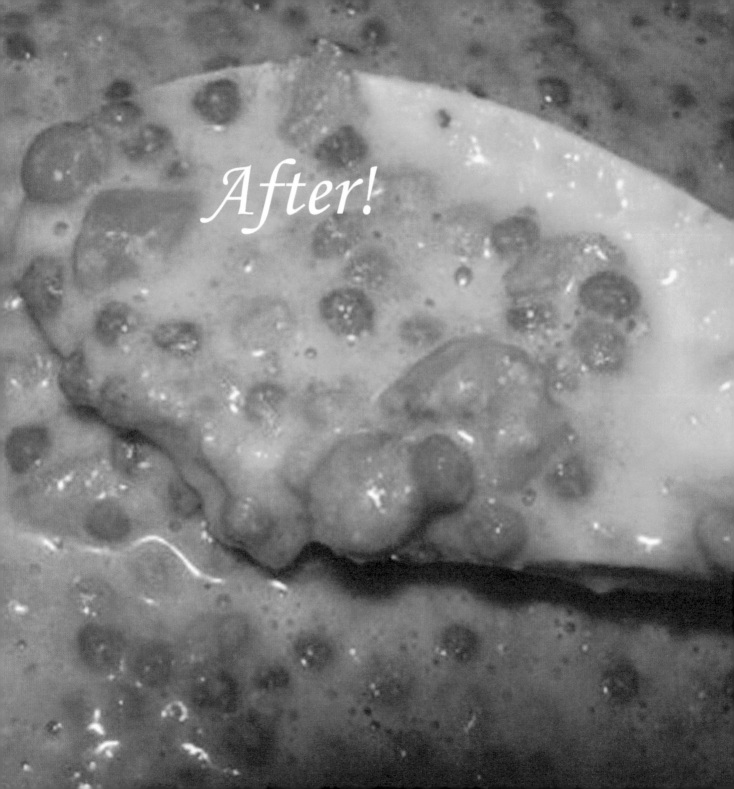

Kimchi

Kimchi is a traditional relish, often made with cabbage. It's similar to German sauerkraut but spicier, and is served with many Korean dishes. It takes a while to prepare, but once ready it can be kept for several weeks.

You will need

1 Chinese cabbage
3 tablespoons salt
around 6 green onions, chopped
3 garlic cloves, finely chopped
½ teaspoon crushed dried hot red chilli pepper
1 teaspoon chopped ginger root

Directions

Cut the cabbage into half-inch strips and soak in salted water for 5-10 hours. Drain, then combine the cabbage with the salt, green onions, garlic, chilli and ginger. Mix well and spoon into a large jar. Cover and refrigerate for 1-2 days before using. Serve as relish or salad.

Cabbage Kimchi

You will need

1 lb cabbage (Chinese varieties work best)
½ tablespoon salt
1 tablespoon spring onions, chopped
1 clove of garlic, crushed
½ tablespoon chilli powder
3 tablespoons soy sauce
3 tablespoons rice vinegar
2 teaspoons sugar

There are lots of different varieties of kimchi. In North Korea it's almost as common a sight as the beloved leader's face beaming from state-controlled TV. It takes a while to make, but you can store it for up to two weeks and use it as either a side dish or a cooking ingredient.

Directions

Chop the cabbage fairly coarsely, then sprinkle the salt over it and leave for 5 hours. Mash it with your fingers after this to make it even softer, then drain off any liquid. Add the rest of the ingredients, then put the mixture in jars, make sure they're well sealed and store them at room temperature for a day or so before eating.

Korean Vegetables in Batter

You will need

1 potato
1 aubergine
some courgettes
some carrots
1 green sweet pepper
3 oz plain white flour
5 tablespoons water
2 eggs, beaten
a pinch of salt

Directions

First make the batter by beating the flour, water, eggs and salt. Next, chop the vegetables; slice the potato and aubergine thinly, cut the carrots and courgette into strips and, with the pepper, use your imagination. Coat them in a little flour before dipping them in the batter, then drop them into half an inch of hot oil to fry them. Serve with a little soy sauce to dip them into.

Rice and Prawn Soup

Directions

Cover the uncooked rice with cold water, leave it to soak for 20 minutes, then drain well. Heat the sesame oil in a large pan, add the prawns and rice wine and sauté gently for 2-3 minutes, stirring slowly. Next add the rice and mix it in well for another 2 minutes. Add about 2 pints of water and season generously. Bring it to the boil, then reduce the heat, cover and simmer for 25 minutes or until the rice is very soft and the mixture has thickened.

You will need

6 oz white rice
1 tablespoon sesame oil
6 oz cooked prawns
1 tablespoon cheongju or Korean rice wine (Japanese rice wine, sake, will also work)

Korean Barbecued Pork

Directions

Chop the spring onion and garlic finely. Mix all the ingredients together in a bowl and leave the pork to marinate overnight. Put the meat on skewers and grill or barbecue until it's crispy round the edges.

Bibim Kooksu

This is a kind of spicy noodle salad. Using Korean wheat flour noodles is the authentic way to do it, but any variety of noodle will do.

You will need

1 large cucumber
6 oz kimchi (spicy cabbage: you can buy it ready-made, but making your own isn't too difficult. See page 106)
1 tablespoon soy sauce
1 tablespoon sesame oil
1 clove of garlic, crushed
1 teaspoon sesame seeds
splash of white vinegar
1 tablespoon sugar
1 packet of dried noodles

Directions

Slice the cucumbers lengthways into long shreds (use a potato peeler, if you have one). Combine the cucumber, kimchi, soy sauce, sesame oil, garlic, sesame seeds, vinegar and sugar, and give them a thorough mix. Cook the noodles in boiling water, then run under cold water and drain them. Add the noodles to the salad mixture and toss it all roughly together. Serve it chilled.

Korean Dumplings

These are a little tricky to make, but it is worth the effort, if you can be bothered. Serve them hot, with a dipping sauce of vinegar and soy sauce.

You will need

4 oz white flour
½ teaspoon vegetable oil
1 egg
1 packet plain tofu
6 oz kimchi (Korean spicy cabbage)
6 oz mushrooms (oriental varieties are best)
4 spring onions
2 cloves of garlic
1 tablespoon sesame oil
½ teaspoon black pepper
1 teaspoon salt
1 teaspoon cayenne pepper

Directions

First make the dough, by mixing the flour, vegetable oil and egg. Add 3 tablespoons of water and a pinch of salt, then knead with your hands until the dough is smooth. Now stick it in the fridge for half an hour while you make the stuffing. Put the kimchi, mushrooms, spring onions and garlic in a food processor for a minute or so until they're finely minced. Sieve the mixture to drain out any excess liquid, then drain the tofu too.

Combine all the stuffing ingredients in a mixing bowl and blend them thoroughly. Roll the dough out thinly and cut into squares about 2 inches across. Place a dollop of stuffing in the centre of one square, dab a little water round the edges and then pinch the edges together to form a little parcel. Steam the dumplings for 10 minutes (you can fry them if you prefer).

Korean Stir-fried Rice

This stir-fry is usually served with kochujang, a Korean hot sauce.

You will need

1 oz beef, cubed
2 oz kimchi (Korean spicy cabbage)
sesame oil
2 oz cooked white rice
2 oz seasoned soybean sprouts
handful of spring onions
2 teaspoons sesame seeds
2 cloves of garlic

Directions

First, mince the spring onions and garlic together with a tablespoon of sesame oil in a food processor. Add the sesame seeds and the bean sprouts, and leave to marinate for a few hours. Chop the kimchi finely. Heat some sesame oil and stir-fry the beef until it starts to brown. Next add the cooked rice and the kimchi and stir for a couple of minutes. Add the marinated bean sprouts, and season well. Don't let the bean sprouts cook for too long; when they're heated through, it's ready to serve. Eat with kochujang if you're brave enough.

キムチ 物語

Dwenjang Jjigae (bean paste stew)

You will need

4 tablespoons bean paste (it's a brown goo made of soya beans)
1 onion, chopped
½ block tofu
1 courgette, sliced
sesame oil
2 cloves of garlic, chopped
1 chilli pepper
2 spring onions
1 teaspoon red bean paste
1 pint stock (vegetable is best)

Directions

Chop the chilli pepper finely and gently fry it in sesame oil with the onion and garlic to release the flavour. Add the bean paste and stir. Next add the stock and bring to the boil before adding the red bean paste. Add the sliced courgette and simmer for 5 minutes. Add the tofu, cut into one-inch pieces, and give it another 2 minutes. Lastly, chop the spring onion (including the green bits) and sprinkle it over the dish just before serving.

Cuba

Cuba's khaki-clad president, Fidel Castro, turned eighty in 2006 and is officially the longest-serving leader in the world. Or is he ...?

Conspiracy theorists insist Fidel has already died, to be replaced by one of his many doubles. Well, possibly. But whoever that bloke with the cigar and beard is, he remains as much a thorn in America's side as the real Castro ever was. Quite some achievement, considering the Commandante has consistently been getting up America's nose ever since he took power in 1959. Overthrowing the corrupt Batista government, Castro and his revolutionaries quickly instituted a Marxist regime, nationalised industry and, yes, even abolished Christmas.

None of this endeared him to his neighbours just ninety miles away to the north. It was all downright un-American! Worse was to follow, as the crazy despot then proceeded to build one of the best health, welfare and school systems in Latin America. Clearly he had to be stopped before Cuba's dangerously low infant mortality rate and high level of education could spread, domino style, to destabilise central America. The US wasted no time in breaking off all diplomatic and trade ties, and began a stand-off that would last for the next four decades. In 1962 they came within a whisker of blowing Cuba off the map over the little matter of some Soviet missiles spotted heading for a silo on the island.

Castro admits to having slept with over 1,000 women.

Then there was the infamous Bay of Pigs affair, when US armed forces had landed in Cuba, fully expecting to start a popular uprising and be heralded as liberators. Unfortunately the Cubans hadn't read the script and the welcoming hordes failed to materialise. The mission ended in humiliation and the Kennedy government had egg all over its face. They must have liked the taste though, since the US subsequently sponsored hundreds of other unsuccessful military incursions into Cuba in an effort to topple Castro. There have also been an estimated 637, that's six hundred and thirty-seven, assassination attempts on Fidel. Everyone's heard of the exploding cigars and the poison pills, but there were also the more bizarre bids to infect Castro's diving suit with a lethal fungus, and to cleverly disguise a bomb as an underwater mollusc. Someone at the CIA has been watching too many Bond films, clearly. But, despite these elaborate attempts on his life over the years, Castro is still clinging on to power.

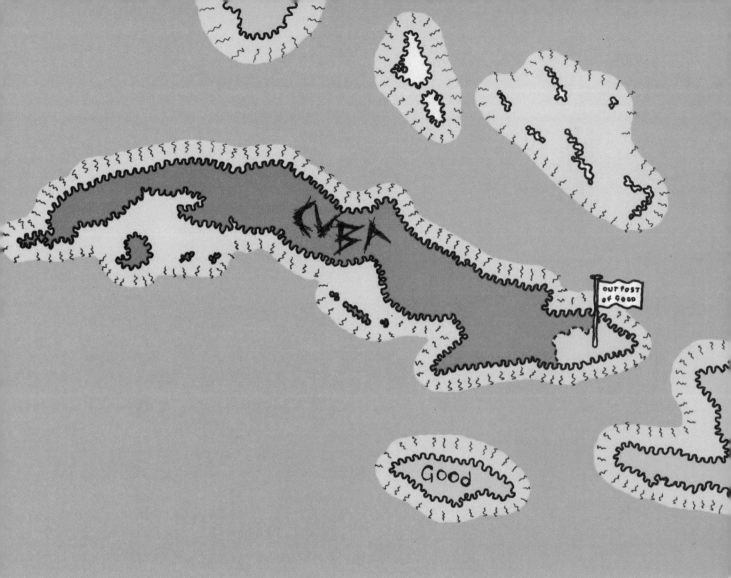

Yep, Fidel is certainly one tenacious dictator. Still, George W. is determined to succeed where others have failed, and is pinning his hopes on economic sanctions: exploding molluscs might not have worked, but there's always good old starvation. Until the 1980s, Cuba's trade with its communist allies ensured relative immunity to the effects of the US trade embargo, but once the collapsing Soviet Union pulled the plug it was a different story. Since then, chronic shortages have been a feature of life in Cuba. In 1994 it entered what the government termed a 'special period', although it's doubtful the experience has been very special for ordinary Cubans, who've had to endure food rationing, power cuts and a nose-dive in their standard of living. Crime, the black market, corruption and prostitution are rife.

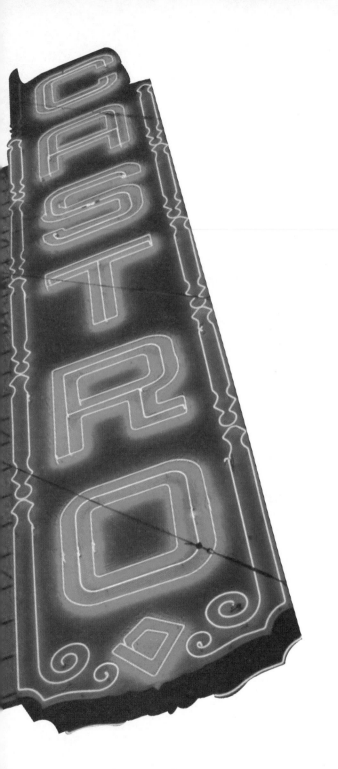

Cuba's poverty has led to allegations that the US trade ban is inhumane. Criticism of the embargo by meddling do-gooders like Steven Spielberg and the late Pope John Paul II is unlikely to give George W. Bush too many sleepless nights, though. In fact, he's cranked up US hostility to Cuba, adding it to the list of Axis of Evil countries in 2003. A special 'Committee for Assistance to Free Cuba' has been established, and even more money pumped into the anti-Castro TV and radio stations beamed from Florida to Cuba across the Gulf of Mexico. Frustratingly, viewing and listening figures seem to have plummeted of late. Um ... maybe it's down to the fact that they don't have any electricity, George? So much for joined-up thinking.

Saddam Hussein used to have his favourite Havana cigars shipped from Cuba by Castro.

Well, no matter: once the repressive Castro regime is deposed, Dubya hopes he can liberate all those political dissidents imprisoned without trial in Cuba. Oh, hang on, maybe not quite all of them. The ones in the orange boiler suits probably won't be going anywhere soon. Guantanamo Bay, the American naval base on the remote eastern edge of Cuba, is of course home to Camp X-Ray, the notorious detention camp for terror suspects and all manner of evil-doers, conveniently situated beyond US jurisdiction so that its inmates can be held indefinitely.

So the economic sanctions are biting, but are the Cubans coming round to Bush's point of view? Not as long as Castro is in charge, that's for sure. He may insist that his leadership is not a personality cult, but it sometimes seems that Castro's charismatic presence and inexhaustible revolutionary zeal are all that is holding communist Cuba together in the face of global pressure to change. In fact, Cuba is not so much a one-party state as a one-man state.

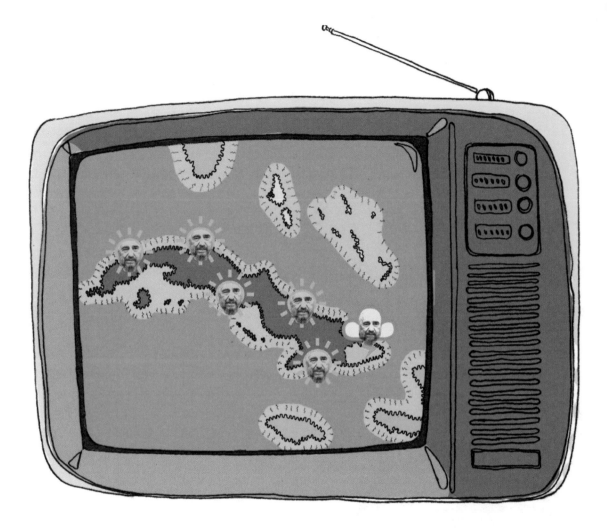

The tireless octogenarian, still clad in his army fatigues, takes a very hands-on approach to government, overseeing every detail of policy implementation, and carrying out negotiations at all hours of the day and night. And in contrast to camera-shy Kim Jong-Il, Castro is all over Cuban TV: not only does he deliver speeches and harangue his own politicians in televised debates, but he sometimes even fronts the weather forecast.

Still, at least there's an 'off' button on the TV: in real life, Fidel's speeches can last up to seven hours, which is surely long enough to test the stamina of even the most committed evil-doer. You can't have too much of a good thing: that seems to be Fidel's motto, at least. He's reported to have fainted in the middle of one such marathon diatribe, but returned to finish it after a brief rest.

But as with most eighty-year-olds, health worries have become more frequent for Castro. In 2004 he fell while presiding at a graduation ceremony, breaking an arm and a leg. Instead of taking things easy, he appeared on TV in plaster to assure his people he was still very much in charge. More seriously, in 2006 he suffered intestinal bleeding, and was forced to hand over the reins temporarily to his brother Raul. Health scares have inevitably produced speculation about how imminent the Commandante's demise is, and what Cuba's fate will be in his absence. Raul, no spring chicken himself, is due to take over power, but without the energy of its iconic president, will the Castro regime crumble? His opponents certainly hope so, and the Cuban community in Miami wait impatiently for his death, placing bets on when he will smoke his last cigar.

The tenacity with which Castro clings to his presidency suggests that he, too, thinks things might change in his absence. As the forces of global capital encroach on communist Cuba, his position is increasingly entrenched. He refuses to make any concessions to the market; the economic reforms that were instituted in the 1990s have largely been revoked, and Castro's hostility is directed against the 'new rich'. While other OAPs might be winding down in their retirement years, and perhaps occupying themselves with a spot of gardening, Castro declares that he's prepared to die with a gun in his hand rather than see Cuba become another 'neo-colony' to the US.

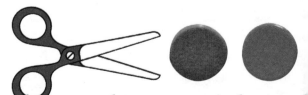

Why not put down your oven gloves and have a game of Snakes and Ladders?

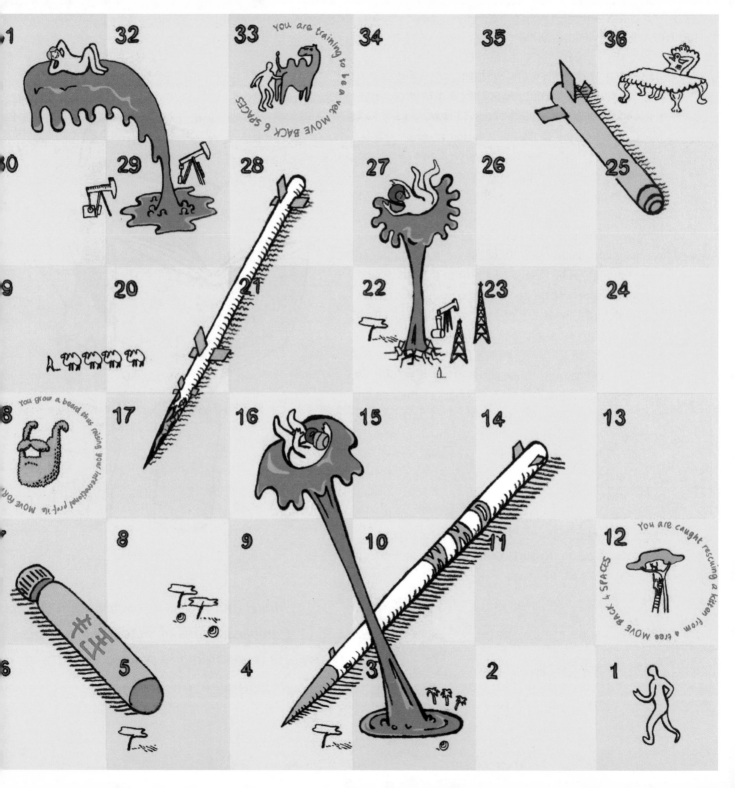

He's certainly not mellowing with age, then. But Castro still has time for a life outside politics. A man who enjoys his food almost as much as he enjoys the writings of Karl Marx, Fidel's favourite dish is reported to be turkey. Or omelette. Or lobster. Or turtle soup. (Could there be something in these conspiracy theories about Castro's lookalikes after all?) His approach to food is every bit as hands-on as his approach to politics, and he has been directly involved in the production of foie gras pâté and special high quality milk. Don't invite him round for dinner though, as he's likely to barge into the kitchen and demand to supervise the cooking (at various times Castro has held forth about the correct way to fry bananas, roast pumpkin seeds and cook lamb cutlets).

Fidel's tastes may run to lobster and foie gras, but his citizens are unlikely to find such delicacies on their ration cards. Since food rationing was introduced to cope with shortages, ordinary Cubans have had to be extremely resourceful to make anything remotely appetising from their weekly allowance of potatoes, rice and meat substitute. And during the 'special period' a TV cookery programme was introduced to help them do just that. It dispensed invaluable advice on how to prepare baked potatoes, mashed potatoes and mouth-watering desserts made out of ... that's right, potatoes. Yum.

Model and political commentator, Naomi Campbell, is one of Fidel's biggest fans. He is, according to Naomi, 'a source of inspiration to the world'.

Whistling in Cuba is punishable by live burial. With snakes!

But it's not all bad news on the gastronomic front. The dire economic situation has led to an unexpected culinar y renaissance in Cuba. Since 1991 a host of semi-legal restaurants have opened in ordinary people's houses. These tiny *paladares*, offering Cuban home cooking and only a few tables, have proved extremely popular and some have attracted an international reputation as well as a high-profile clientele. These days it seems you can't move in Havana without bumping into the likes of Jack Nicholson, eager to sample the delights of 'new Latin' cooking.

Christians and Moors

There are lots of different variations of this, as it's one of Cuba's most famous recipes. It comes from Spain originally and the title is a reference to the Muslim Moors of North Africa who once controlled part of Spain. Rice versus black beans: yep, it's Bush's War on Terror on a plate!

You will need

½ lb white rice
1 onion
1 green bell pepper
3-4 cloves of garlic
½ teaspoon chilli powder
1 can chopped tomatoes
chopped coriander
½ lb black beans (Sometimes called black turtle beans. You can buy them dried in health food shops.)

Directions

Prepare the black beans. If they're dried this usually involves soaking them overnight and then boiling them for an hour in the morning. When they're slightly soft, drain and set aside. Put the rice on to boil until it's soft and fluffy, and while that's cooking fry the chopped onion along with the chopped pepper and garlic. Add the chilli powder and then, when it's all starting to soften, pour in the tomatoes and simmer for about 10 minutes over a low heat. Add the beans and let them heat through. Mix the bean sauce into the rice and serve, sprinkled with coriander. Keep the leftovers and you can stage a re-enactment of the invasion of Operation Iraqi Freedom, using the medium of food.

Black Bean Hummus

Hummus, that staple dish of the Middle East, is also found in Cuba, proving beyond any doubt that the Axis of Evil countries have been sharing their sinister snack-making technologies! In Cuba they don't use chickpeas but black beans, so if you have any left after making Christians and Moors, try whipping up some of this.

You will need

cooked black beans (Black turtle beans. If you buy them dried, follow preparation instructions on the packet.)
1 tablespoon tahini (sesame paste, available in Middle Eastern shops and health food shops.)
2 cloves of crushed garlic
1 tablespoon lemon juice
salt and pepper

Directions

Mix all the ingredients together in a blender until smooth. Serve with bread or salad.

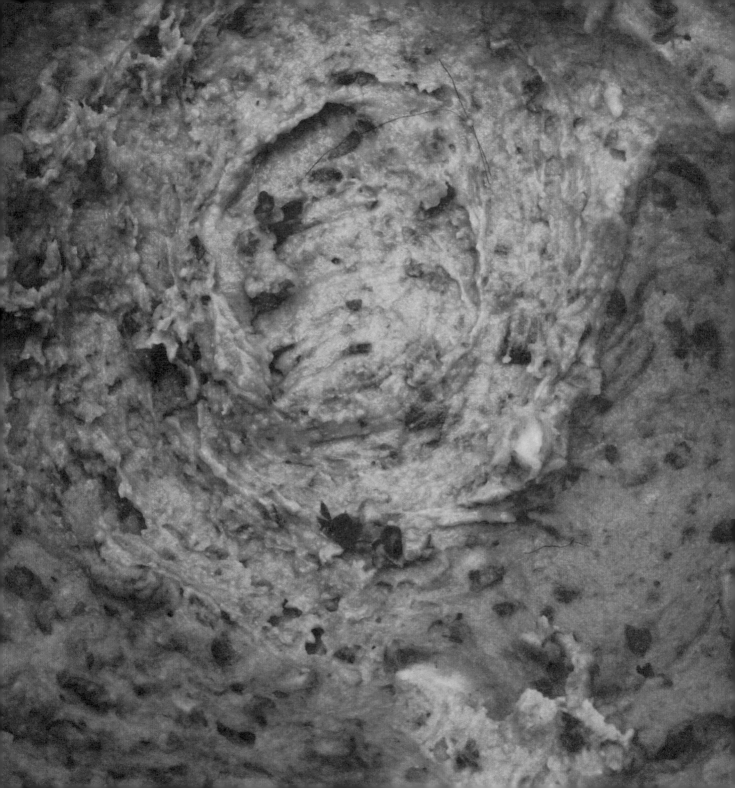

Crushed Potatoes

You will need

new potatoes: as many as you fancy
olive oil
1 onion
fresh parsley

Directions

Boil the new potatoes in their skins in salted water for 15 minutes or so. Drain and set aside for a few minutes. Pick one up in a kitchen towel and squeeze it gently between fingers and palm until it's slightly crushed. Now do the same with the rest, and fry them in medium-hot oil for 5 minutes, turning them to ensure they crisp evenly. way through, season and serve as a side dish.

Boniatillo (sweet potato dessert)

What better to follow a potato-based main course than a potato-based dessert?

Directions

Boil the potatoes until soft, then mash them. Heat the sugar, with some water and the lime zest, in a saucepan, adding a teaspoon of cinnamon, stirring all the time until it becomes syrupy (should take about 15 minutes). Then add the potatoes and stir the mixture over a low heat for another 5 minutes. Add the beaten egg yolks and the rum and stir for a couple more minutes. Remove from the heat, transfer to dessert dishes and put them in the fridge for a few hours. Sprinkle some cinnamon on the top before serving.

You will need

about 1 lb sweet potatoes. You're supposed to use the Cuban variety of white sweet potatoes, but if Cuba is more than a bus ride away then you can use any sweet potatoes you can find. The pink ones are fine.
grated peel of 1 lime
ground cinnamon
3 egg yolks
½ lb sugar
splash of dark rum

Fried Plantains

You will need

some plantains

Directions

Peel and slice the plantains into ½ inch thick slices. Fry them. That's it.

If you can't get hold of plantains then fry some bananas instead.

Ajiaco (meat and veg stew)

Intelligence sources claim this is Cuba's national dish. But can we believe them?

You will need

roughly equal quantities of the following, all in about ½ inch cubes:

pork
beef
pumpkin
boniatos (Cuban sweet potatoes)
squash
corn
name (yam)
yucca
plantain

N.B. Some of these may not be easily available. To get that authentic taste of Cuba in the 'special period', substitute all the ingredients with potato.

You also need a pint and a half of beef stock, lime juice and a spicy tomato sauce called sofrito. For the sofrito chop an onion and a green chilli pepper finely and fry them in oil and garlic. Add a tin of chopped tomatoes and a pinch of cumin. Simmer for 10 minutes.

Directions

In a large saucepan, cover the meat in stock and simmer over a low heat for about an hour. Then add the vegetables, add more liquid to cover them if necessary, and cook for another hour. When all ingredients are soft, add the sofrito, lime juice and chopped plantain if you have it. Cook for another 10 minutes and serve with rice.

Arroz Frito (fried rice)

You will need

cooked white rice (43,578 grains)
2 eggs, whisked
½ lb diced ham or shrimp, or you can use both
5 chopped spring onions
2 teaspoons chopped garlic and ginger root
soy sauce
chopped coriander

Directions

Lift out of the pan and slice into strips. Repeat until the egg mixture is used up, then put more oil in the pan and fry the rice with the garlic and ginger. Add the ham, shrimp and spring onions and stir. Add the soy sauce (and some chilli sauce if you like) and finally toss in the egg strips. Sprinkle with the coriander and serve.

Tocino de Cielo (heaven's bacon)

You will need

5 egg yolks, whisked with a splash of water
½ lb sugar
vanilla extract

This is actually egg custard. Who knows why it's called bacon? Castro, probably.

Directions

First coat the bottom of a metal mould or baking tin with sugar and hold over the heat until it melts to form caramel. Then put the rest of the sugar in a pan, pour in enough water to cover it, and heat until it turns into syrup. Remove it from the heat and pour it slowly into the egg yolks while stirring constantly. Pour the mixture into the metal tin. Now either steam it for an hour (place the tin in a colander over some boiling water) or put in a moderate oven for about 50 minutes. When the pudding is set, let it cool in the fridge before serving.

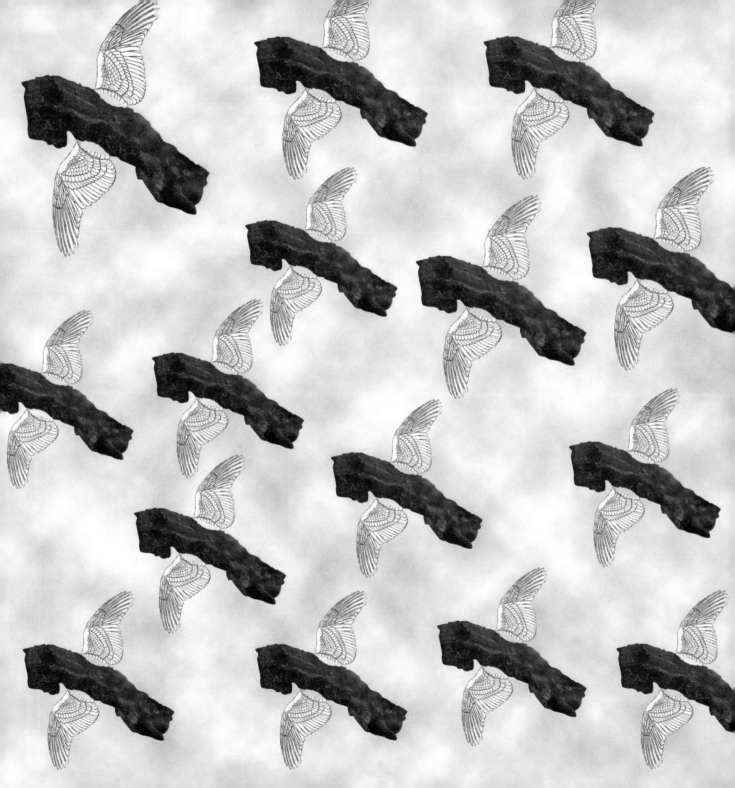

Avocado and Pineapple Salad

Directions

Dice the pineapple and avocado and mix together in a bowl. Add a dressing of lime juice, sugar, salt and finely chopped onion. You can also throw in some lettuce.

You will need

1 avocado (ripe but not too soft)
½ pineapple
1 small onion
lime juice
sugar
salt

Sounds weird. Tastes quite nice.

Fried Cow

You will need

2 lbs steak (ideally flank)
2 bay leaves
6 peppercorns
3 tablespoons dry sherry
2 tablespoons olive oil
2 onions
2 green peppers, cut into slices
1 lemon
And for the seasoning, mix together some chopped garlic, black peppercorns, ground cumin and salt.

Directions

Just cover the steak with water in a saucepan and add the bay leaves and peppercorns. Put the lid on and simmer for about an hour and a half, or until tender. Allow it all to cool down, ideally overnight. Slice the meat into serving size pieces. Cubans tend to pound it with a meat mallet at this point, but then they have a lot of pent-up aggression, what with the shortages. Rub each piece with a bit of the seasoning and splash with dry sherry.

Now heat the olive oil in a frying pan, and fry each piece of meat until it starts to turn brown. Add the onions and peppers to the pan along with the meat. Then serve it up with lemon pieces as a garnish.

This one's made out of cow, fried. It's OK. You don't need a whole cow.

Frita (Cuban hamburger)

In yet another demonstration of un-American behaviour, Cubans have subverted the good old hamburger. Those Godless commies have their own version. This is enough for four.

You will need

1 lb ground beef
1 egg
a large pinch of paprika
2 fluid oz milk
1 dollop each of mayonnaise and ketchup
a generous handful of breadcrumbs
a small amount of finely chopped onion

Directions

Combine all the ingredients and then shape into burger-sized balls. Let them sit in the fridge for a couple of hours, then fry them in oil, slightly flattening them with a spatula. Serve in a bun and contemplate the end of capitalism as you eat.

Libya

So is Libya in the Axis of Evil or not? Even Washington doesn't seem sure. In 2003 it was declared a 'rogue state' and included in an expanded list of Axis countries ...

But international enmities, just like friendships, can be fickle and just three years later this policy was revised by the US, who reinstated full diplomatic relations in May 2006. The roots of Libya's unpopularity with the West go back much further than this to the 1980s, when it was considered a major terrorist threat. The destruction of Pan Am Flight 103 over Lockerbie in 1988, which killed 271 people, was alleged by the US to be the work of Libyan agents. After it refused to hand over the two men accused of the bombing, Libya was subjected to harsh economic sanctions from the early 1990s, and these have only just been lifted.

The recent thawing of relations with the West has a lot to do with the eventual successful extradition of the two agents for trial, and also with Libya's agreement to pay compensation to relatives of the victims (whether Libya has officially accepted responsibility is a thorny issue, however). But what really underlie Libya's fluctuating relations with the West are the caprices of its mercurial, maverick leader, Colonel Muammar Gaddafi.

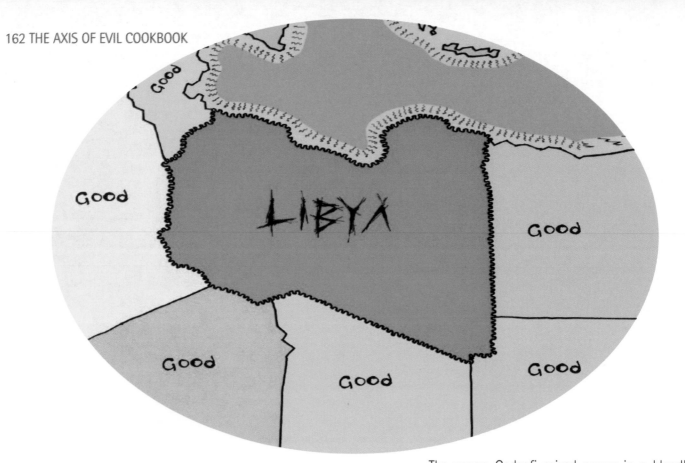

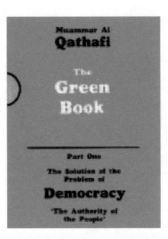

The young Gadaafi seized power in a bloodless coup in 1969, overthrowing a weak monarchy largely under the control of Western economic interests. Establishing a new republic, snappily named 'Jamahiriya al'Arabiya al-Libiya ash-sha al-ishtrakiya', he proceeded to ban alcohol, close down the US and British military bases and nationalise the newly discovered oil fields, using the oil revenues to fund what is probably the most comprehensive education and welfare system in the Arab world. A self-styled visionary and thinker, Ghadafi expounded his political philosophy at tedious length in the Green Book, and the Libyan government is run according to the logic-defying principles of his 'third universal law'.

DECLARATION
NOTICE TO ALL AFRICAN PEOPLE

The Brother Leader Col. Muammar Al-Qaddaffi, the leader of the Libyan Revolution, calls all the Africans to move immediately in all parts of the continent without passing the gates and facing the complex procedures that obstruct the transport access, in order to carry out the contacts between the African groups and to solve the demographic balance in the continent.

He also calls for neglecting these illusionary borders, recognizing that such borders had been and are still the cause of all the sorrows the continent is facing including the civil wars and other different problems.

So, the Leader calls upon all the Africans to move freely from one country to another from 02/02/2002, which is an unrecurring history but after one thousand years. Let the Africans move freely without a visa.

Aligning itself with neither communist nor capitalist ideology, Libya is a 'state of the masses' or Jamahiriya, meaning that decisions at every level are made by an elected people's congress. Whether the result is a socialist utopia or repressive dictatorship depends on who you ask, but an honest answer might be hard to get from Libyans themselves, since critics of the government can face imprisonment with no right to a public trial. The press is controlled by government, and newspapers have been closed down for making seditious comments. Elected congresses exist alongside an un-elected government run by - guess who? - Gadafy. Despite having no official title as head of state, he still maintains ultimate control. Political parties are not permitted to exist and 'The Leader', as he is known in Libya, deals ruthlessly with his opponents, in 1979 ordering the public hanging of dissident students.

In the Western world, meanwhile, he may be a copy-editor's nightmare (there are thirty-two spellings of his name), but Qaddafi is a mediaman's dream and his colourful statements and eccentricities have generated acres of newsprint and hours of TV coverage, especially in the 1980s when he was the dictator the West loved to hate.

Muammar Qaddafi, Mo'ammar Gadhafi, Muammar Kaddafi, Muammar Qadhafi, Moammar El Kadhafi, Muammar Gadafi, Mu'ammar al-Qadafi, Moamer El Kazzafi, Moamar al-Gaddafi, Mu'ammar Al Qathafi, Muammar Al Qathafi, Mo'ammar el-Gadhafi, Moamar El Kadhafi, Muammar al-Qadhafi, Mu'ammar al-Qadhdhafi, Mu'ammar Qadafi, Moamar Gaddafi, Mu'ammar Qadhdhafi, Muammar Khaddafi, Muammar al-Khaddafi, Mu'amar al-Kadafi, Muammar Ghaddafy, Muammar Ghadafi, Muammar Ghaddafi, Muamar Kaddafi, Muammar Quathafi, Muammar Gheddafi, Muamar Al-Kaddafi, Moammar Khadafy, Moammar Qudhafi, Mu'ammar al-Qaddafi, Mulazim Awwal Mu'ammar Muhammad Abu Minyar al-Qadhafi.

FROM DODGE CITY TO TRIPOLI

HIS GUNS WERE THE ONLY LAW!

RONALD REAGAN

LAW and ORDER

Color by Technicolor

Dubbed 'the mad dog of the Middle East' by President Reagan, Khaddafi appeared to positively enjoy getting up Washington's nose, allying himself with pretty much every cause likely to strike fear into the hearts of Western governments. In the 1980s, it seemed that the Libyan Desert was a veritable terrorist training ground, as Kadafi demonstrated his support for the IRA, the PLO, the Black Panthers and the Sandanistas, as well as playing host to other figures unlikely to be on America's Christmas card list, like Nation of Islam leader Louis Farrakhan and Ugandan dictator Idi Amin.

These days Gaddafi has become something of an icon, and has even had an opera written about him.

An alleged sponsor of international terrorism and an all-round bad guy, Quathafi has been a target of numerous assassination attempts. American fighter planes attacked his compound in Tripoli in 1986, in response to the bombing of a Berlin nightclub in which US servicemen were killed. Included in the 100 fatalities was his adopted daughter, but Gadafy is made of stern stuff and, despite the machinations of his enemies in the West, has outlasted no less than six US presidents and retains a firm hold on power in his country.

Al-Quadhafi has never been afraid to make bold statements, even when they make no sense whatsoever. He managed to unite both Arabs and Zionists in outrage with his recommendation that the Israel/Palestine problem should be solved by the creation of a state called 'Israetine', and confidently declared that 'the fifty million Muslims of Europe will turn it into a Muslim continent within a few decades'.

On the subject of sexual health too, Gheddafi has held forth, declaring that heterosexuals 'have nothing to fear from AIDs'. Some of his health advice can be difficult to follow, though. Here he is on the dangers of watching sport: 'addicts of the football are the first to be hit by the psychological and nervous sicknesses leading to angina pectoris, strokes, diabetics, blood pressure and early senility. At the time when movement of a human being constricts due to excessiveness of technology use; and accordingly becomes lazier, more exanimate and flabbier.'

Al-Saadi has also played for the Udinese football team, after supposedly buying his way into the Italian league.

Qadhdhafi has always cultivated his own individual style of Bedouin-chic. Clad in flamboyant robes and hats, he cuts a dash wherever he goes, surrounding himself with his 'Amazon Squad', a forty-strong all-female troop of uniformed (and allegedly virginal) bodyguards. He knows how to make an entrance too, and reportedly attended a summit in Belgrade riding a white charger.

But however ostentatious his behaviour, Kezzafi still likes to remember his humble nomadic roots in the North African desert, and has been known to take a herd of camels on his international travels to provide milk. And even when undertaking state visits in his private jet, he always sets up home in his traditional Bedouin tent.

*G's glamorous daughter Ayesha, dubbed the
'Claudia Schiffer of North Africa', was one
of Saddam Hussein's defence lawyers.*

*Rumours abound that Gaddafi's
son, Al-Saadi, has dated
Hollywood actress Nicole Kidman.*

MOR soul crooner Lionel Ritchie recently sang at a 'concert for peace', commemorating the American bombing of Tripoli (how much suffering can the Libyan people take?). And if Qadhafi's musical tastes are a bit middle-of-the-road, it seems that his politics are heading that way, too. The mad dog now receives visits from Tony Blair and is a staunch opponent of Islamic extremism; he was the first and most vociferous Arab leader to condemn the 9/11 attacks and to denounce Al-Qa'ida. He has also allowed weapons inspectors into the country and announced the end of his nuclear ambitions, a fact that George Bush was keen to attribute to the fear of ending up camped out in a hole like Saddam Hussein.

Whether this change in attitude is due to worries about US military intervention, a desire to make peace with old enemies or the financial temptations on offer from Western oil companies, is something only the wily and inscrutable colonel will ever know. But now that waging armed struggle on the forces of imperialism takes up less of his time, he is free to pursue more sedate pastimes like honing his literary talents, and has published a volume of short stories.

Ever the gentleman, Gaddafi famously broke wind loudly (and apparently deliberately) several times in a 1988 interview.

Gaddafi

Lionel Blair

Tony Blair

'Three degrees of separation ...'

His other forays into the world of letters are on the Net: unafraid to embrace the new, the sixty-five-year-old Ghadaffi keeps his people in touch with his thoughts through a website and his personal blog. And on the evidence of these, though his politics might be mellowing in his old age, his ego remains as robust as ever. 'The existence of Al-Qadhafi is closely related to the historical development of humanity itself,' declares his website, since he is 'justly considered as the leader of his epoch, as an upholder of the rights of the persecuted, of the oppressed and humiliated, and of all those rejected by society'.

Shakshouka

Variations of this dish are found all over North Africa. It's tasty and it's super-easy to make.

You will need

1 red sweet pepper
1 green sweet pepper
3 cloves of garlic
3 tomatoes (a tin of chopped tomatoes will do)
a pinch of cumin
1 green chilli pepper
1 onion
4 eggs

Directions

Chop the onion, garlic, sweet peppers and chilli pepper, and sauté them in a medium-sized frying pan along with the cumin. When the vegetables start to soften, add the tomatoes, finely chopped, and simmer over a medium heat for about 5 to 8 minutes, stirring occasionally. You can add tomato purée or paste for some extra tomatoeyness. Now break the eggs into separate corners of the pan (do pans have corners?) and then cover. When the eggs are cooked but not hard it's ready. Dish it up onto plates, or alternatively serve out of the pan with slices of crusty bread.

Basbousa (semolina cake)

Basbousa is a semolina cake found across much of North Africa. This variation has yoghurt in it but you can make it without if, for example, you don't like yoghurt.

You will need

a pile of a blanched almonds (bigger than a ping-pong ball but not so big you have to build an extension to your kitchen). Finely chop most of them, but leave about 10 whole to decorate the cakes.
5 oz fine semolina
3 oz sugar
½ pint yoghurt
6 oz butter
1 teaspoon baking powder
1 teaspoon vanilla essence

For the syrup:
7 oz sugar
¼ pint water
a generous squirt of lemon juice

Directions

Make the syrup by heating the sugar, water and lemon juice. Don't forget to stir it, and take it off the heat when it becomes sort of, um, syrupy.

While it cools, busy yourself by chopping some almonds, then cream the butter and sugar together in a mixing bowl. Sift in the semolina and baking powder, add the yoghurt and vanilla and give it a good old mix. Spread the result into a shallow greased baking tray and arrange the almonds evenly on the top (there should be one for each piece of cake when it's sliced). Put it in a medium oven for about 20 minutes, or until it feels springy when pressed. Pour the syrup over the top, allow it to cool and then slice and serve with cream.

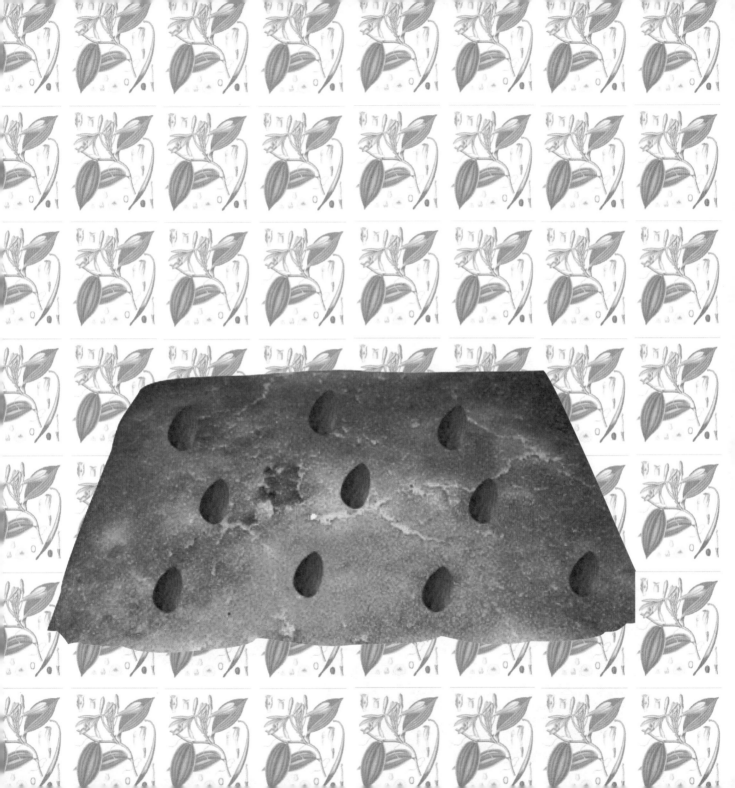

Mhalbiya (rice pudding)

This is a smooth version of rice pudding; instead of actual rice, it uses rice flour, which you can find at your friendly local Libyan supermarket, or failing that, a health food shop.

You will need

1 pint milk
4 heaped tablespoons rice flour
3 oz sugar
3 tablespoons 'atr, or extract of geranium. If you've run out of extract of geranium, you can use rose water. If you don't have any rose water, you'll just have to imagine what it would taste like.

Directions

Heat most of the milk together with the sugar in a saucepan over a gentle heat. Add the remaining milk bit by bit to the flour, stirring all the time to ensure a smooth paste. Add this to the pan, again gradually, stirring constantly until it starts to boil. Add the 'atr, or whatever substitute you're using. Pour into small dishes and refrigerate. Decorate with cinnamon and almonds before serving.

Aubergine and Pepper Salad

You will need

2 large aubergines
1 red sweet pepper
2 crushed garlic cloves
the juice of half a lemon
1 onion, finely chopped
breadcrumbs (You can buy these ready made, unbelievably. Or you can make your own, using bread.)

Directions

Bake the aubergines and the pepper for at least 30 minutes, or until the skins start to wrinkle and crisp. Put the aubergines in whole, but chop the pepper into thickish strips. Wait for them to cool, then peel the aubergines and mash the insides with a fork. Peel the peppers too, and chop them more finely before adding them to the aubergine flesh. Now add the breadcrumbs and the remaining ingredients, give it another mash and put it somewhere cold. A fridge, for example.

Halwar Lamr (sugared dates)

Directions

Mix the dates, figs and honey to a rough paste (use a food processor if your Bedouin tent is equipped with one) and then mix in the nuts. Form into balls and roll them in the sesame seeds so they're coated evenly.

You will need

8 oz stoneless dates. Some of this quantity can be made up with figs, but they need to be fairly soft.
chopped nuts (almonds are best)
1 tablespoon honey
sesame seeds

Phœnix dactylifera.

Date. Fruit.

Date.
Fruit cut vertically.

Date. Seed.
Face opposite
chalaza.

Date. Seed.
Face opposite
hilum.

Date. Seed cut transversely
(mag.).

Date.
Embryo (mag.).

Stuffed Peppers

You will need

4 medium-sized sweet peppers (any colour will do)
1 large onion
1 clove of garlic
1 small green chilli pepper
cooked rice (2 handfuls should do. That's assuming your hands are the size of mine.)
2 tomatoes, chopped
1 can chickpeas
a pinch of paprika
cinnamon

Directions

Chop and sauté the onion, garlic and chilli pepper. After a couple of minutes add the chickpeas, rice and tomatoes, along with the spices. Stir and simmer for 5 minutes or so. Slice the tops off the sweet peppers and hollow out the insides. Fill with the rice mixture and put the tops back on. Place them in a flat oven-proof dish with half an inch of water. Bake for 50 minutes, or until the water is gone and the peppers are tender.

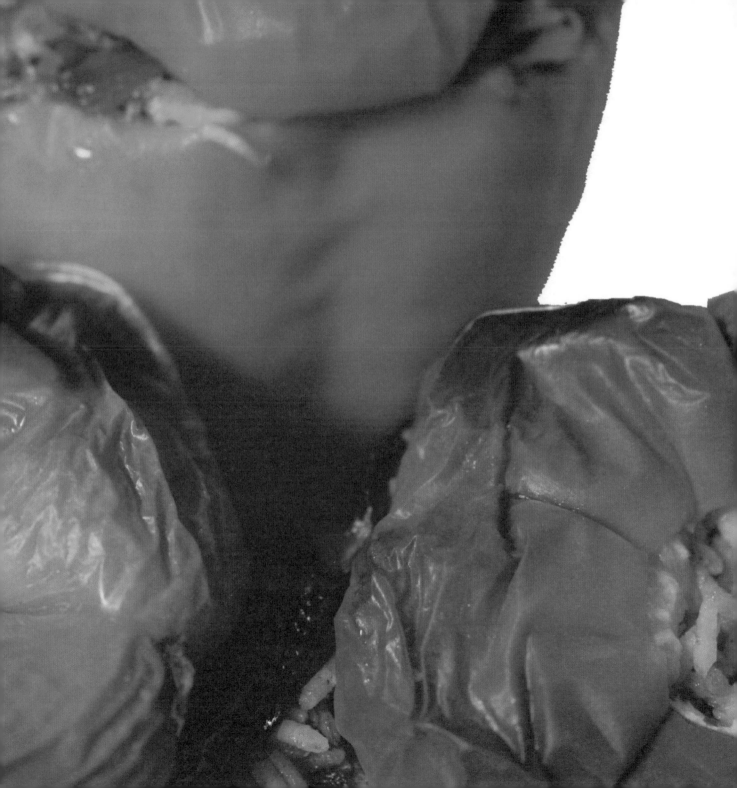

Vegetable Couscous

Couscous, coarsely-ground semolina grains, is such a staple of the North African diet that in many places it is simply referred to as ta'am or 'food'. This is a kind of tasty Libyan fritter, ideal as a side dish.

You will need

couscous
2 cloves of crushed garlic
grated root ginger (2 teaspoons of powdered will do)
2 bay leaves
4 chopped tomatoes
1 green chilli pepper
2 carrots
1 courgette
2 medium potatoes
harissa sauce (if you don't have this, substitute a teaspoon each of paprika and cumin)
1 medium chopped onion

Directions

In a large cooking pot gently sauté the garlic, onion, ginger and chilli pepper. Then add the tomatoes and bay leaves and cook for another few minutes. Now add the rest of the vegetables, roughly chopped, and a teaspoon of harissa (careful, it's hot, remember). Pour in enough water to cover the ingredients, bring it to the boil and then leave to simmer. Meanwhile, measure out enough couscous for however many people you're feeding (there should be enough vegetables for four) and place it in a colander lined with a clean tea towel. Stick it over the simmering vegetable stew, cover with a lid and leave it to cook.

Mint Tea

Mint tea, or atay, is drunk all over North Africa, often amid much elaborate ceremony involving silver teapots and the like. If Colonel Ghadaffi ever pops round and you're a bit stuck for what to serve him, just make him some of this. There should be enough for him and about half of his Kalashnikov-toting Amazonian Guard.

You will need

Directions

Warm the teapot first (ideally it should be metal). Into the pot, put 1 tablespoon of green tea, and a generous handful of whole, fresh mint leaves, including the stalks. Add boiling water, and a few teaspoons of sugar, according to taste. Allow it to brew for 5 minutes, stirring occasionally, then pour into small cups. You can add more sugar at this stage if you like.

Eijjat

This is a kind of tasty Libyan fritter, ideal as a side dish.

You will need

1 large courgette
1 onion
2 tablespoons flour
1 tablespoon baking powder
1 teaspoon chilli powder
a pinch of salt and pepper
2 eggs
fresh coriander

Directions

Finely chop the courgette, coriander and onion, mixing them thoroughly with the flour, baking powder, chilli powder and seasoning. Add the eggs, beaten, and give the mixture a good squish with your hands. Form into golf-ball-sized pieces and then press them down slightly with a spatula as you fry them in hot oil. When they start to turn crispy and golden they're ready.

Sharba Libya (Libyan soup)

You will need

1 medium sized Libyan ... no, it's not THAT kind of Libyan Soup, silly.
½ lb lamb, cut into small pieces
1 large onion
1 tablespoon tomato purée
chopped parsley
3 tomatoes
1 lemon
generous amounts of salt, paprika and cinnamon

Directions

Gently fry the onion with the meat in oil. Add the parsley and the tomato purée, along with the chopped tomatoes, the salt and the spices, and stir energetically. Add enough water to cover the meat and simmer until the lamb is tender. Add more water if required and bring it to the boil. Sprinkle mint leaves over the soup if you have any lying around, otherwise add a squeeze of lemon and serve it up.

SYRIA

Poor old Syria. While its fellow rogue states North Korea and Iran are busy striking terror into the hearts of God-fearing Americans, Syria is a teensy bit anonymous and, well, just plain boring, if we're honest ...

accountant

dictator

The main problem is its leader. Other evil despots are easy to spot in their familiar Mao suits, military fatigues or crazy robes, but Syrian president Bashar al-Assad favours a sensible suit and tie (and, after all, could a man who looks like he shops at Burton's really bring the Western world to its knees?).

Where Kim Jong-Il and Colonel Ghadaffi may have the unmistakable air of ruthless dictators, Bashar has the unmistakable air of a chartered accountant. Or to be more accurate, an

optician, since if he wasn't harbouring and facilitating global terror, 'Dr Bashar', as he is known to his countrymen, would probably now be working in Specsavers. Having trained in London, he was heading for an unremarkable career as an eye doctor when his elder brother Basil, at that time being groomed for power, was killed in a car accident. Bashar was suddenly catapulted into the limelight as the new successor to his father, the altogether more notorious figure of Hafez al-Assad, and on the latter's death in 2000 Bashar became president.

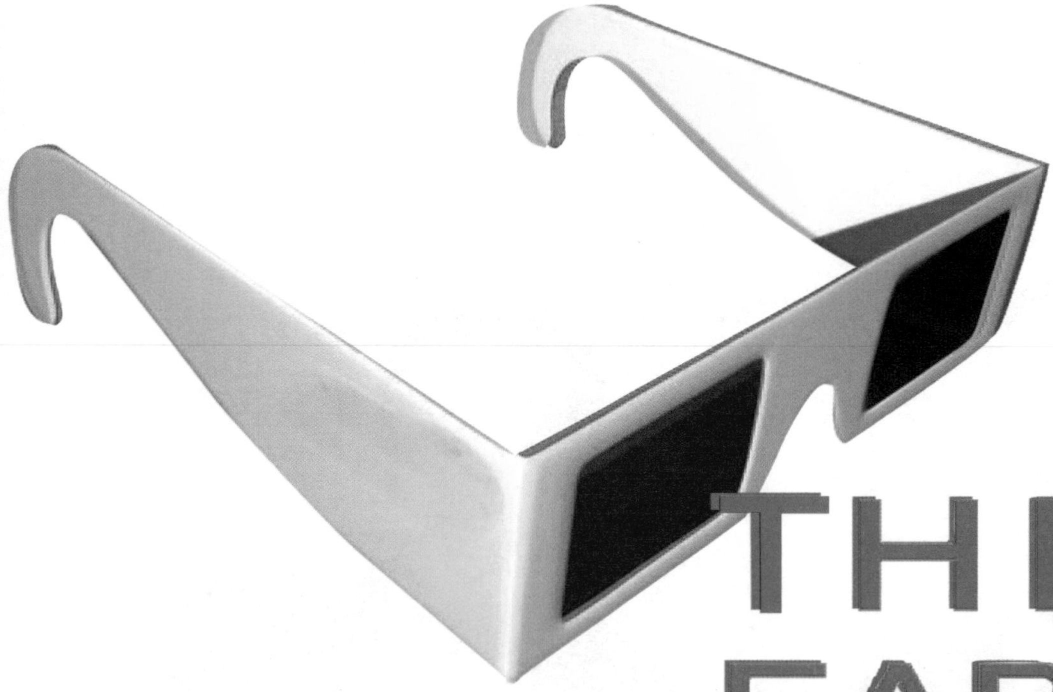

THEW
EAPON
SOFMA
SSDESTR
UCTIONARE
HIDDENAT

. . . .

Assad senior died having ruled the country since 1970. Like any self-respecting despot he originally took power in a military coup, and swiftly got on with doing the things evil-doers are expected to do. Like having himself re-elected every seven years with 99 per cent of the vote, getting rid of political opponents and generally being ruthless. His eradication of the Sunni Muslim brotherhood resulted in the massacre of 10,000 people in the town of Hama and effectively silenced any potential opposition.

Much like the publicity-shy Kim Jong-Il, Hafez al-Assad was hardly ever seen in public but nevertheless exercised almost total control of his citizens, restricted press freedoms to a minimum and severely punished any dissent. He had all the hallmarks of a ruthless dictator, but it wasn't his human rights violations that interested Washington so much as his supposed involvement in terrorism. Washington accused Damascus of being behind some of the major terrorist attacks of the 1980s: an infamous bomb attack on an American base in Beirut which killed over 250 soldiers as well as the 1985 hijacking of a TWA airliner in Lebanon.

Coca-Cola is not available in
Damascus. That's how evil it is.

So much for Assad the dad. The presidency of Assad junior seemed to herald a new, more open and altogether less evil era for Syria. The 'Damascus Spring' of 2000 saw the release of hundreds of political prisoners and the start of the first independent newspaper in more than three decades. The country's creaking economy, once closed to any outside influence, was slowly opened up and for the first time in decades private banks and a stock market were permitted.

There are now government-run Internet cafés in Damascus, and wealthy Syrians can also at long last enjoy that mighty and potent symbol of cherished and time-honoured American values, the doughnut. A Dunkin' Donuts franchise (owned by a cousin of the president) has opened on the border with Lebanon, and the oppressed citizens of Syria may now experience previously undreamt-of freedoms in the form of obesity and heart disease. It's enough to bring a tear to your eye.

Syria is the birthplace of the olive.
They were first cultivated there some 5,000 years ago.

However, any expectations that Syria was about to embrace Western-style capitalism and democracy were short-lived. Aside from some cosmetic reforms the Syrian political and economic climate remains much as it was. For most Syrians, especially the ones who can't afford doughnuts, the reality of life remains one of poverty and unemployment in an economy plagued by corruption and nepotism. The press is still restricted, as is Internet access, and any anti-Syrian websites are banned. More importantly, as far as George W. Bush is concerned, Syria continues to be a veritable hotbed of evilness, and stands accused of supporting terrorist groups including Hamas, Islamic Jihad and, of course, Hezbollah. This last group has become the real bone of contention between Damascus and Washington, implicated as it is in Syria's clashes with Israel and its longstanding involvement in Lebanon.

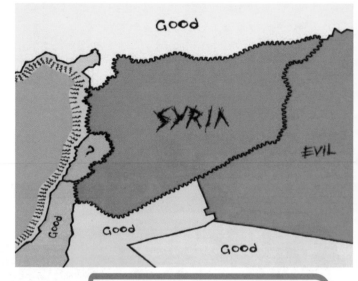

A buffer state between Syria and Israel, Lebanon was occupied by Syrian forces in 1976. The occupation was initially justified as a peacekeeping mission to keep warring Christian Maronites and Palestinians apart; but the Syrian army then forgot to go home, and just sort of stuck around for the next twenty-nine years, much to the annoyance of Israel. The assassination of former Lebanese Prime Minister Rafik Hariri in early 2005 brought this Syrian presence to an end. The finger of guilt was pointed at Damascus, who denied any involvement but sheepishly withdrew Syrian troops from Lebanon.

Tensions didn't ease, though. The following year saw incursions into Israel by Lebanese-based Hezbollah soldiers, and heavy bombardment of Lebanese territory by Israel. As the death toll mounted and fighting threatened to spiral out of control, President Bush was on hand to provide an incisive analysis of the situation. Bush knows evilness when he sees it; it wasn't Hezbollah or even Israel who were at fault, but those terror-sponsoring Syrians up to their old tricks. Chomping noisily - possibly on a pretzel - Dubya eloquently summarised the situation for the benefit of Tony Blair: 'What [the UN] need to do is get Syria to get Hezbollah to stop doing this shit and it's over.'

Syria is twice the size of Scotland, but only has a fraction of the number of Scottish people.

Dr Bashar enjoys Pilates and crosswords.

The Syrian national anthem is Total Eclipse of the Heart by '80s soft-rocker Bonnie Tyler.

So it seems that, despite his mild-mannered appearance, Dr Bashar has done his best at times to live up to his father's evil reputation, especially when it comes to Israel, with whom Syria has been at loggerheads ever since Israel borrowed the Golan Heights in 1967 and just never gave them back. Bashar is unlikely to get an invitation round to Ariel Sharon's anytime soon; not since his 2001 speech in front of Pope John Paul II, in which he compared Israel to the Nazis, and stated that Jews had betrayed Jesus Christ and had tried to betray and kill the prophet Mohammed. Israel has returned the favour, sending war planes over Assad's coastal residence in Latakia at 3 AM and letting off a sonic boom.

Given such repeated stand-offs with Israel, it looks unlikely that Syria will be leaving the Axis of Evil anytime soon. In 2004 the US turned up the heat, imposing sanctions, demanding Damascus end its support for 'Palestinian terrorist groups' and cease its pursuit of Weapons of Mass Destruction. Hawks in Washington have been calling for military intervention in Syria. However, while President Bush may be stupid, he isn't that stupid; Assad may be evil, but he is possibly the lesser of two evils as far as the West is concerned. Anti-American sentiment and support for Hezbollah among Syrians is high, but the rise of fundamentalist militia in Syria is held firmly in check by the secular Ba'athist regime. If the example of Iraq is anything to go by, such groups could prove difficult to deal with once the totalitarian regime is toppled.

And, of course, let's not forget that while Syria might have lots of pesky evil-doers, one thing it doesn't have much of is oil (or anything else, for that matter; Syria is a relatively poor country in terms of natural resources). This 'evil to oil ratio' reduces Syria's overall evilness quotient, putting it somewhere near the bottom of the list of rogue states due for some good old US-style regime change.

For someone with no discernible personality, President Assad seems to be surrounded by one heck of a personality cult. His besuited image adorns huge posters all over Damascus. Indeed, he appears to be a very popular man, if the amount of pro-government demonstrations is anything to go by. These spontaneous demonstrations are scheduled on a regular basis. Demonstrators, who have invariably had the foresight to carry around banners bearing Assad's image, chant touching declarations of loyalty to their president, such as 'Assad, our spirit and our blood are yours'. Participants are often carried to the rallies in buses belonging to the president's tycoon cousin. For those who've been paying attention, that's the same one who owns Dunkin' Donuts. (Yes, the Syrian regime is certainly one big happy family. Or one big nepotistic and corrupt clique, depending on your point of view: the Assads' fellow Alawite sect predominate in government and at least twelve of Bashar's immediate relatives are powerful and wealthy figures.)

Of Dr Bashar himself, relatively little is known and despite his huge wealth he seems to live unostentatiously. Perhaps he likes nothing better than to loosen his tie - just ever so slightly - and enjoy an outing to his cousin's doughnut emporium. Or he may eat traditional Syrian cuisine, which has the reputation of being the best in the Middle East. However, his years of training in London, during which he reportedly dined in NHS staff canteens, may have withered away his tastebuds to the point at which he is no longer able to enjoy or even taste food. Who knows?

Lahum Nee (raw beef)

This is a very simple appetiser and, after all, what could be more appetizing than raw beef?

You will need

½ lb ground beef
1 onion
chopped coriander
pitta bread
salt and pepper to taste

Directions

Chop the onion finely and squish all the ingredients together with your hands, along with some salt and ground pepper. Serve it up with some pitta bread, and turn the TV over if there's one of those BSE stories on the news.

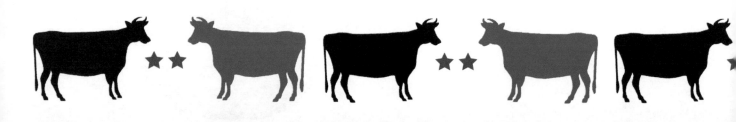

Sheep Kidney Toast

You will need

1 lb sheep kidneys
a pinch of parsley
1 onion
3 tablespoons butter
a generous splash of Worcestershire sauce
2 tablespoons flour
a pinch of salt and black pepper
breadcrumbs
sharp cheese (feta would work well)

Directions

Split the kidneys in half, peel off the outer skin and remove any sinewy bits. Mince it finely, in a blender unless you're feeling energetic. Add the parsley and onion to some melted butter in a pan and fry for a few minutes. Add the Worcestershire sauce. (You can't buy Coca Cola in Damascus, but apparently you can buy Worcestershire sauce. Strange.) Sprinkle with flour and cook for a couple of minutes, before stirring in the flour. Now add the kidneys, salt and pepper and then spread the mixture over thin slices of toast. Cover with the breadcrumbs and finally a layer of cheese. Enjoy.

Mujadarra, or lentil pottage, is so old it's mentioned in the Old Testament; Esau sold his birthright for some. Make your own, keep hold of your birthright, and serve it as a side dish with pitta bread.

You will need

cup of red lentils
cup of burghul wheat
2 onions
1 teaspoon cumin

Directions

Sauté the onions in oil until tender, then remove from the oil and drain them. Next add the lentils to the hot oil, soaking them first if necessary. When they start to brown, add water (about four times the amount of lentils) and bring to the boil, stirring to make sure the lentils don't stick. Now add the burghul wheat and simmer for 20 minutes, until lentils are tender and most of the liquid is absorbed. Stir occasionally, adding more water when necessary. Spoon the rice mixture onto a serving platter, then sprinkle with the fried onions.

Shish Kebab

Apart from those alleged arms supplies to Hezbollah, Shish Kebab is probably Syria's best-known export. It's ideal for the barbecue and can be made out of pretty much any combination of meat and vegetables.

Directions

Marinate the meat in olive oil, lemon juice, salt and pepper for a few hours. On skewers, arrange the meat, alternating it with the peppers, aubergine and onion. Stick it on the barbecue or under the grill, turning regularly until the meat is tender and browned.

You will need

½ lb lamb, cut into ½ inch cubes
2 onions, cut into quarters
2 green pepper, cut into strips
2 aubergines, cubed
5 tomatoes, halved
lemon juice

Tabbouleh

The trick to making this is to chop everything finely.

Directions

Cook the burghul wheat according to the instructions on the packet, and allow to cool. Add it to the chopped parsley, mint, tomatoes and spring onions. Add the pepper and lemon juice and drizzle with olive oil. Mix it thoroughly and add salt to taste.

You will need

parsley. Absolutely loads of it.
fresh mint. Quite a lot.
about 3 spring onions
2 tomatoes
burghul wheat. About a mugful should do.
the juice of 1 lemon
1 teaspoon black pepper

Felafel

You will need

1 can chickpeas
1 onion
3 cloves of garlic
1 teaspoon salt
1 teaspoon cumin
1 teaspoon ground coriander
1 teaspoon baking powder
2 teaspoons flour
a pinch of chilli powder
fresh parsley

Felafel is ubiquitous in the Middle East. It's delicious, and less likely to give you a heart attack than a burger. Serve it hot with pitta bread and hummus.

Directions

Put all the ingredients in a food processor and mix until they form a stiff paste. Shape into golf-ball-sized pieces and fry in hot oil until evenly browned and slightly crispy.

Hummus

Chickpea-based snacks are extremely popular with vegetarians and evil-doers alike. Yes, you can buy it, but making your own is more fun.

Directions

Give the chickpeas what for in a food processor for a minute or so, then add the other ingredients. Switch the processor back on and while it's doing its thing, gradually add water to it until the paste reaches a creamy consistency.

You will need

1 can chickpeas
the juice of 1 lemon
3 tablespoons tahini (sesame paste)
a pinch of salt
2 cloves of garlic
2 tablespoons olive oil

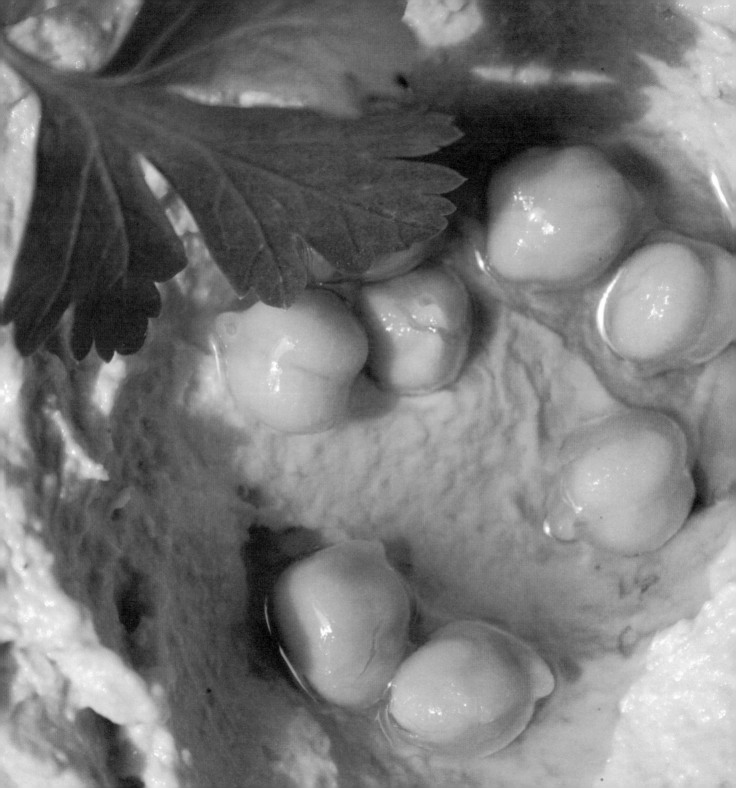

Baklava

This dessert can be found in many outposts of tyranny, showing a high degree of cooperation between the Axis of Evil countries.

Directions

Mix walnuts together with the sugar, cinnamon and cardamom for the filling. Melt some butter in a pan and spread about a quarter of it in the bottom of a baking dish. Put one sheet of the filo pastry in the baking tray and brush with some of the melted butter. Repeat until you have about 15 filo sheets in the tray. Now spread the walnut mixture evenly over the pastry. Layer another 15 sheets of pastry over the stuffing, brushing each with melted butter. Pour any remaining butter over the top, then cut into squares. Place in a hot oven for about half an hour, or until the top turns golden. Pour the honey onto the baklava and allow it to soak in. Wait until it cools, then serve.

You will need

a generous handful of chopped walnuts
2 tablespoons clear honey
1 teaspoon cardamom
1 teaspoon cinnamon
2 tablespoons sugar
a packet of filo pastry
2 tablespoons butter

Baba Ganoush

It's a tasty aubergine dip. It's also an anagram of BANG HA USA BOB.

Directions

Bake the aubergine in a hot oven until the skin starts to crisp. Allow it to cool, then peel and mash the contents. Blend the flesh with the other ingredients and mix together thoroughly. Serve as a side dish with pitta bread.

You will need

1 large aubergine
1 tablespoon tahini (sesame paste)
the juice of 1 lemon
2 tablespoons olive oil
2 cloves of garlic
a pinch of salt

Fattoush (toasted bread salad)

You will need

2 cloves of garlic, chopped
a handful of chopped fresh mint
the juice of 1 lemon
olive oil
1 loaf pitta bread
6 romaine lettuce leaves torn into smallish pieces
1 diced cucumber
2 diced tomatoes
2 spring onions, chopped
1 diced sweet red pepper
1 can chickpeas, drained
1 teaspoon salt
1 teaspoon pepper

Directions

For the dressing, mix the garlic, salt, pepper, mint, lemon juice and olive oil. Toast the pitta bread, then break it into one-inch pieces. Put the bread, romaine lettuce, cucumber, tomatoes, green onions, bell pepper and chickpeas in a bowl and mix with a spoon. Drizzle the dressing mixture over the salad and serve.

Lentil Soup

You will need

dried red lentils. Enough to form the outline of very tall Syrian leader Bashar al-Assad, if laid end to end.
1 onion, chopped
1 teaspoon cumin
4 teaspoons flour
a handful of cooked rice
2 tablespoons olive oil
a pinch of salt
a sprinkling of black pepper
1 red sweet pepper, diced
the juice of half a lemon
2 tablespoons finely chopped parsley

Directions

Add the onion to the lentils, along with the flour, rice, oil, sweet pepper and seasoning. Add enough water to cover, then bring to the boil, watching carefully to ensure that it does not overflow. Reduce heat and simmer, covered, for 40 minutes, adding more water when necessary to keep it liquid, but not too thin. Pour into a processor and blend until creamy. Add lemon juice to taste, parsley and extra olive oil.